From The Spiritology Series of Self
Help/Spiritual Growth Manuals:

THE POWER
OF
SPIRITOLOGY

Volume I

By Dario Thomas: Copyright
12/26/2011

The Misconception of Spiritual Growth:

There is a common misconception about spiritual growth. Many see it as a continuous journey that never ends. It is commonly taught that you die (experience physical death) before you can reach the plateau of the spiritual heights. This viewpoint, however truthful it seems, is totally false. Christ taught the very opposite. Much like the body, the mind, and the spirit can grow into adulthood. God designed everything to work according to parallel laws: meaning that the spirit grows into maturity just like the body. The irony of it all is that you are born into the world with a true Godly spirit. But because of naiveté, the new born individual slinks and recoils into mental dungeons. They become prisoners of their very own negative viewpoints and mindsets. This book gives you a way to escape the dungeons. It shows you how to release the shackles of fear and re-obtain your initial God given spiritual freedom. Keep in mind the spiritual journey is riddled with many errors and blunders for the one that wishes to be free. However, with it comes a miraculous capacity to recognize the mistakes, coupled with the desire and motivation to not repeat those mistakes. Therefore be encouraged, read and study the book; faithfully practice the techniques and watch yourself grow. It is a truly magical process that will indeed amaze you.

May all the blessings of the Supreme God be upon you.

Table of Contents:

Book VII:

Book VIII:

What is Spiritology?

Spiritology is the latest of emerging religions that actually provide: the missing keys of the Kingdom: the final element of salvation. That is consciousness.

Spiritology defined is the study of the spirit: "Spirit" (as defined per Spiritology) is the being, the self, or the "I" of the person. It is that self that exists independently of and is the operator of the mind and body. Spirit is the eternal point of conscious awareness of the individual. The suffix "ology" defined is a branch of learning or study: the study of; therefore, Spiritology can be considered the study of the spirit or self: spiritual study, or self study.

About this manuscript:

This book may seem judgmental at times: especially when referring to organized Christianity, and organized religion in general. If this is the impression that you get, then I would like to ask that you take time out to set aside the ego, reflect upon what was read, and allow Truth to be revealed to your spirit. If you are still offended by the material, then I would like to take this time to apologize in advance. In general, this book is written in the masculine but applies to male and female alike.

This book may seem unorganized or like a series of random put together subjects, if so, it is because it was written in the sequence that the words and ideas came to me; however, I feel that everything will come together for the reader as it should once the reading begins and progresses.

This book is not long or of lengthy duration. There are several books out there that will do you a world of good. Books like the "Bible" come to mind. These books, although they are master pieces, and no doubt were written by spiritually awakened men, they are quite lengthy and how many of us have passed up golden opportunities because we were scared off by the number of pages contained in a book. For this reason alone is why many Christians haven't read the Bible from cover to cover. It's considered too large and time consuming. This book gets right to the point of what your life's difficulty is (sense of separation from God) and how to solve it.

Finally, this book may seem repetitive or even redundant when talking about the only issue that the reader has and how to eliminate the issue; this is because the book is repetitive in that aspect. For the most part, the redundancy is its constant reminding you of observing yourself and how to do it. After all, repetition is the mother of skill and a methodology for impregnating your mind with an idea that eventually becomes reality in the material world once the idea is accepted, so read it and partake upon its redundancy.

The goal of Spiritology:

Most religions have the lofty aspirations of transforming the world; and such is to goal of spiritology, but spiritology is catered toward the individual. The goal of spiritology is spiritual rebirth through self correction for the individual. For as Christ once said, "How can you help your brother get a speck out of his eye while there is a beam in your eye? Get the beam out of your eye first and you will be able to see clearly to help your brother get the speck out of his." Spiritology puts no pressure on the individual to recruit the masses or preach to the world that there is a better way. It is not necessary anyway, and as an individual grows spiritually he will understand why. Spiritology only requires that the individual take a good look at himself. Only through careful self observation can an individual develop spiritually. A truly spiritual individual will not have a need to preach or convince another of his way of life because his life will be a living embodiment of all that God meant for mankind to be. His life will be an example that will attract others far more than any salesman-like preaching could ever do. In other words, he will walk the walk as well as talk the talk.

Who Is Spiritology For:

The author's personal intention is that Spiritology should be a wake up call to organized Christianity; Spiritology is for those whom have grown tired of the customary, ritualistic, but useless. It is for those individuals who have finally realized that their traditional ways, thinking, and religious practices have not produced any tangible results. Some of which in spite of their systems have grown even more fearful and bitter toward life and the world. It is for those Christians who constantly march to the altar at least once a year to rededicate their lives to Christ. It is for the true followers of Christ who finally realize that organized Christianity has gone amiss and the now so-called body of Christ has become the very systems that Christ rebuked with regard to the religious hypocrites that made up the church body while He walked the Earth. Spiritology is also for the non-Christian who wishes to experience true spiritual growth. If this is you, then spiritology is for you.

Spiritology mission statement:

God is Omnipresent; therefore, my mind as well as my body is the temple of God, and wherever God dwells, a devil, false ego, fear, or false belief cannot reside.

A typical day:

It starts out with being jarred out of my sleep by an alarm clock. I hit the snooze button at least 2 to 3 times minimum. One of the first thoughts that usually pop into my head is, "I should've gone to bed earlier because I could use more sleep." Then it hits me: feelings of futility and mild despair. I'm not sure what it's about, but it's there, and it creates a struggle for me to even get out of bed. I drag myself out of bed and get myself ready for work; I know that a vague feeling of anxiety will accompany me throughout the day. Once I'm in the car and driving down the road, my mind races with incessant random thoughts which are for the most part stressful and negative. Some of these thoughts are based upon reality from past events or future worries, and some are pure make believe. I hate this process, but I don't know how to stop it. It's an automatic process that is forced upon me day in and day out. I am stressing and imagining about how the day will turn out before I even arrive to work. What am I going to say to or do about people that I despise but pretend I like to their faces? In my imagination, I let them have it once and for all, but in reality I remain pretentious that all is well, and they follow suit. I can tell that they really don't like me either but pretend to also. Sometimes I wonder if they are fooled by my pretentiousness or if they even suspect that I resent them ever so slightly. I am sure they feel the same way toward me. They have to. Its human nature (ego nature). My mind can't seem to help itself. It dwells on the negative. It is filled with hundreds, maybe even thousands of fears. Now I am seeing a debate that I had with my significant other a couple of nights ago. I didn't handle it so well. I said some mean things that hurt her feelings. She in turn responded in a way that made me mad also. First, I am thinking about her snappy retort and envisioning what I should've said back to her that would've vindicated me and at the same time hurt her even more. Maybe I should've called her a choice name along with everything else I said to her. That would've showed her who's in charge. Then, another emotion kicks in: remorse. I call myself an idiot for saying such terrible things to her and imagine making it up to her and telling her that I am sorry for being an idiot. Next, a third stupid feeling jumps on the band wagon: foolish pride. I say to myself, "why should I apologize? After all, she is the one that started this whole mess with her dumb female double standard mentality. She's the one that should be apologizing. I should call her up and break it off right now. That will show her." I convince myself that this is what I will do, and finally fear comes into play. I call off the whole mess, in my head, of course. I can't take the thought of her being in the arms of another man anyway, and since I secretly suspect that she has a backup male friend waiting in the wings (another negative feeling called paranoia kicking in) I don't dare do anything to make her more upset than what she already is because if she leaves me for someone else, I'd be devastated. I then realize that I don't care whether or not we make up, but I make it up to her for fear of seeing another man in her life. That's egotistical human love in a nutshell. Next, I notice the car in front of me hesitates to proceed, once the light turned green; I honk my horn and call whomever it is a not so nice name. My mind then sees a cowcatcher attached to the front of my car, and I indignantly bulldoze the car in front of me off the road and smirk at the other driver in self satisfaction. I arrive to work and that feeling of anxiety that I woke up with is still there. It is down hill from this point on. My mind is on negative automatic pilot and won't give me a break. My life's energy is being constantly drained; every now and then I ask God for help amidst the mental chaos. I manage to get through the day; 5 o'clock comes and relief hits me; time to go home; then that feeling of despair comes back again.

What am I going home to? I have nothing and no one. I am alone in the world. Nobody truly understands me. I feel hopelessly lost. I am lost. I need a miracle. Please God won't You help me? The answer? Silence; the same nothing that I feared has happened again just like every other day. I am now wondering, if God truly hears and answers prayers. What's going on? Why is He giving me the cold shoulder? I'm not asking for fame, fortune, or any other worldly thing; I just want peace of mind. Is this too much to ask? Why hasn't God responded? It's been years now. When will help come? Am I going to have to wait for death? Is the silence of the grave the relief that I want? Sometimes I say to myself maybe death wouldn't be so bad. At least I won't have to deal with this crazy world anymore. All the while I am failing to realize that my own craziness is the major contributor of my personal reality. I won't take my own life, but I ask God that if death is to come, then let it be painless and happen when I am sleeping. Aside from thinking about death, this is a typical day. If your days are similar, and you are tired of arguing and fighting internally, if you are part of an organized religious body and you are tired of pretending that you have rock solid faith just because your peers claim a strong relationship with God (although you know they are in the same predicament as you are) then spiritology is also for you.

Spiritual sleep:

We all know what happens whenever we physically

go to sleep. We become unconscious. Shortly after, we start to dream. I have heard people say that they don't have dreams or rarely have dreams, or don't remember their dreams; I've also heard (so-called) experts (on dreams) say that everybody dreams while sleeping whether they know it or not. Let's consider dreaming for a moment. In a nutshell, dreaming is unconscious mental activity giving the appearance of consciousness. You go to sleep, lose consciousness of the outside (physical reality) world, and your (mechanical/subconscious) mind takes you places. Sometimes these places are in the past and sometimes they're in the future. Sometimes reality is distorted or mocked up. It seems real while it's happening, but afterwards we wake up. Sometimes we awaken naturally; sometimes we are jarred out of sleep by some kind of shocking experience during the dream. Once we wake up, we immediately know that we were dreaming because we are now (consciously speaking) back in the real world (physically and mentally). Upon awakening, we can immediately sense the difference between the real world and the dream world; can't we? Well, I have some heavy news to lay on you. Even while their bodies are up and running in the physical world, men and women all over the place are still unconscious. Think about it. Their minds are still taking them places: to past regrets and pleasantries or future worries and hopeful or dreadful anticipations. And like in physical sleep, their minds are even mocking up realities. This (mechanical) mental activity seems constant and never ending; correct? Yes, they are up and walking around, conducting business, driving vehicles, fighting and warring with each other, and interacting with each other in numerous ways in the present moment, but their minds are somewhere else (in dreamland); therefore (in a way) they are asleep while awake. This is what is known as spiritual sleep, and if you were to truly wake up or somehow get jarred out of it, you'd immediately know the difference. You'd be a truly decent, happy, and optimum functioning human being. The way to wake up is to see that you are asleep.

Differences between spiritual sleep (unconsciousness) and spiritual wakefulness (awareness):

Conscious thought or creative thought and awareness (constant persistent present moment perception) is what a spiritually awake person experiences. Conscious thought (practical thought, constructive thought) exemplifies the mindset of an aware person. Conscious thought is often used as such: assembling a piece of furniture, doing laundry, driving to work, or whatever day to day tasks or duties an individual is to perform. In essence, you are thinking about what you are doing at the moment you are doing it. Creative thought is also employed by an aware person: an artist painting a masterpiece, a musician composing a symphony, or a writer developing a thrilling novel. An awakened person's mind alternates between awareness and conscious thought or creative thought. Negative thought/mechanical thought/ego possession are all indicative of spiritual sleep.

A runaway mind, a mind that incessantly produces compulsive thoughts, imaginings, and noise is mechanical mind. A mechanical mind is a mind that possesses an ego. An ego generated mind has no choice but to produce negative and destructive thoughts. To possess an ego is to be spiritually asleep. A spiritually asleep person's mind alternates between, practical thought, creative thought, and negative/mechanical thought. There is hardly any present time awareness going on or the awareness is dulled and lessened by negative emotion or mechanical mind activity. It is a vicious and energy draining cycle and the only cure is to wake up.

Book I

Spiritual growth is possible.

Communion with God is possible. Walking with God or knowing the Lord is totally possible. Most religious folk claim spiritual growth, but as the years go by, the evidence contradicts their words; they grow more miserable and bitter towards life and other people with the passage of time. Spiritual growth and mental degradation cannot coexist. The main reason for this dilemma is because most individuals truly don't know the difference between their minds and their spirits. An individual cannot grow spiritually, commune with, walk with, or know God with his mind; an individual cannot grow spiritually and at the same time continue to be plagued with mental troubles and ailments. As Jesus Christ said, "those that worship (meaning to know, commune with, incessantly acknowledge, walk with, give praise to) God must do so in truth and spirit; Christ said to do so in spirit, not with the mind. The mind is the den of the devil. With all the neurotic chasings and negative ramblings of the mind that is filled with anxiety and contempt, how can it be used to truly acknowledge God? The Spirit of God will not inhabit an unclean vessel. It is time to redefine the term "spiritual growth." Spiritology is the study of the spirit. This is a paradox because the spirit cannot truly be studied. The spirit can only "be." Since the spirit is the "being" in and of itself, it only makes sense that it cannot be studied. It is the "studier or the "I" of the person. It is the One within that is using the mind and mental processes to study. The mind is used to study by the spirit. It gathers facts and data by observing its surroundings, stores, compiles, and puts together the observed information as memory into an organized body of knowledge. This knowledge is in turn used to handle whatever an individual may encounter in the physical world and mental world. Often times, the body of stored knowledge is negative and faulty. As a result, an individual uses faulty and sometimes even fatal methods to deal with the outer world. Only the mind can be studied and used to study the physical world. A corrupt mind cannot enter into the untainted spiritual realm. Man can only use the mind to study the physical world; he can also introvert or look within and study his mental processes. By studying the workings of his mind, he can unravel the cluster of erroneous beliefs and ideas about himself and the world. It is not necessary to try with mental force to think positive or change faulty beliefs. All that needs to be done is to tell oneself the truth about oneself and study oneself. With patience and due diligence, a man can study the workings of his mind and reignite his original intelligence: the Word of the Lord. It is with his original intelligence (God given instinct and intuition) that a man realizes what faith in God really is and what it can do. It is with his original intelligence that a man can dismiss all fear and uncover his Spirit or Essence of Being that is united with God. At that point all studying ceases, thinking stops, and a man is reborn spiritually. He ceases to think about himself and starts to be himself. Spiritology is a way for a man to rediscover himself and thereby live life victoriously. It is not necessary for a negative minded individual to find out who gave him labels, how his fears developed, or how he got emotionally scarred at an early age. Not only would it be too time consuming, it would be virtually impossible to probe the memory in an attempt figure out the hows, whys, and whats that happened at every given moment in life; he'd probably die of old age before that happened, even if his life's span was a thousand years, but by studying the present operations of his mind and mental processes, a man can be reborn. This I know. I have been reborn and am now growing up within the spirit.

Impartial Self Observation:

This is the only technique that you must practice and master to be successful on the spiritual path. It is the ability to separate your conscious center of awareness (the real and untainted "I" which is the center of your being) from its mental absorption and use it to look at what is going on inside and outside of you. With this faithful, persistent, and non judgmental watching (especially of the inner mental turmoil and unrest) you will gradually and systematically dissolve the false/ego self. By watching yourself inside and out (and this part is crucial) without getting afraid or upset with what you see, you will eventually achieve enlightenment. The special exercises in this book are designed to assist you with contacting your untainted "I." Faithful practice of one or more of the exercises will result in your mind being cleaned up; it will clean up to the point of where you will no longer need to do the exercises but will have enough clarity to perform impartial self observation at anytime in any place; start wherever you are and take the next step. Throughout this book you will be given hints and pointers as to how to observe and what to observe about yourself. Practice makes perfect.

What Spiritology is not about:

Spiritology is not about hypnotism, mental conditioning, or mind programming. It has nothing to do with cults or the occult. The exercises in this book were carefully tested by the author: mostly on himself. It doesn't directly encourage positive thinking or changing your belief system. What it does do; however, is start a process of un-conditioning, deprogramming, and dehypnotizing the mind. It is a system for stripping away all the harmful labels and ideas that have for so long been ruining your life. Once this is done; you revert back to pure insight and guidance from God. The way to accomplish this is to recognize the false personality within that is currently controlling your life and allow the True Personality to be reinstalled as the frontrunner of your life.

The two you's:

You have a dual personality. There is a Real You and a false you. The Real You is one with God. It knows no fear because it realizes that everything and everyone is in and of God. It knows that all is one. The false you is who you imagine yourself to be. It thrives on mental associations and comparisons. It believes in separation, duality, good and evil. The false you keeps its position by constantly comparing and associating itself with people events and objects outside of itself. It identifies with just about everything, even God and the devil. The false you has conned you into believing that it is a real entity but it is purely imagination. All of your fears, phobias, worries, jealousies, hopes, neurosis, psychosis, and every other negative state, have attached themselves to the false you because of these comparisons and associations. It has tricked you into believing that you have multiple issues and problems, but in reality, you have only one problem, and that problem is the false you. Get rid of this fake id, and you simultaneously get rid of all other issues. The way to get rid of this fake id is by contacting the Real You. The Real You only needs your recognition and permission to evict the false you. Recognizing the Real You is achieved by first recognizing the false you. When you see that you are not the imaginary you or the egotistical you, then the Real You surfaces and works its magic with no effort on your part. It reclaims its position in your life by supplanting the false you.

The Real Self must be contacted:

You may have tried or at least heard of many self-help programs. More than likely, if you have tried any of them, you may not have followed through, and if you did, then the results probably were not what you expected. In other words, you were let down. The problem with many of these programs is that they tend to be complicated. They go something like this: 10 steps to a better you or 7 days, 21 days, 30 days to a better life. Another problem is that you have to overcome negative human nature in order to follow through. Even the programs that try to show you how to motivate yourself or think positive are complicated in the same ways. If you have to follow a step by step program then chances are you won't succeed. Your negative human nature is too powerful to resist, so you fall short. You have to already be positive in the first place in order to think positive, but no one considers that. If it wasn't for the fact that your negative nature keeps thwarting your attempts at motivation then there would be no need for any type of program. You could simply change yourself whenever you felt like it in an instant just like you would make the bed every morning without any painstaking effort. Also, these motivational programs are catered to the false you or the ego self. This is why they are doomed to failure. It is the ego self that is attempting to find motivation, direction, a life's purpose, or even a relationship with God. Bet you didn't expect that last one. A false entity cannot have a relationship with a real God. Real self-help is not complicated at all; it can be done at your own pace, and it doesn't require a series of complicated steps. You only need to do one thing. You need to watch yourself. You need to see yourself as you really are and stop lying to yourself. Well, I guess that could be considered two things. You can watch how your mind continuously races with random thoughts and images, distorts or replays events, is always getting sucked into past happenings, make believe, future worries, mocked up versions of past events, and fantasies. If you watch consciously, then that is all you need to do. That is the only cure and the only real self-help. Conscious seeing, without fretting, worrying, or being judgmental about what you see, is all that is necessary to end all of your woes. Just like you can't cure yourself when you cut your finger, you can't mentally cure yourself either, only God can cure you; your job is to get out of the way and allow the cure to take place; this is very easy but also easier said than done. You have to train yourself to see consciously; see with your Real Self. Man has made the mistake of believing that he can mentally cure himself for too long already. This is why the list of psychotic conditions continue to grow year after year. Man must drop his arrogance and put things in proper perspective. Man must get himself out of the way and allow God to do His work.

Knowing God:

The average individual who claims spirituality fools himself about knowing God. This is a very hard pill to swallow, but as soon as a man takes his medicine regarding this fact is when true spiritual and mental healing begins. An individual may have been taught perhaps in church or wherever about what God does and who God is. He has been told stories since he was a child about the miracles of

God, most notably in the Bible. He has been given examples in modern life from faithless people about God's divine intervention. He has been given an idea of God and an imaginary picture of God, and he is now convinced that "it", his imaginary picture, is the Real Thing. This idea is housed in the imagination and wreaks havoc in his personal life. The reason being is because he doesn't even know that he has the idea of God instead of the Real Thing; a false idea will never come to your aid, deliver you from evil, or answer your prayers; there is something else at work going on in a man's mind that he is equally unaware of. He has also developed an imaginary self, self image, or an ego. The ego is purely imagination just like his idea of God. His ego is who and what he imagines himself to be but not his Real Self. His ego (imaginary self) has taken over his very existence and is causing all his problems. It is because of the ego that he feels separated from God and all of Life. Whenever he prays to God, calls upon the name of the Lord, or even tries to commune with God, he fools himself. This is because it is not the Real Man that is trying to make contact. The real Man doesn't have to. The real Man is already connected. It is the imaginary man doing the praying or supplicating. The imaginary self is the one creating misery and simultaneously suffering from its self created misery. This imaginary self is not only doing the praying, but it is praying to the imaginary idea about God. Imagination is praying to imagination. A fake man is petitioning a fake god, the prayer doesn't rise above his mind, and as a result, nothing constructive happens. He starts to wonder if God has even heard the prayer. He starts to imagine how and when the answer will come. He even worries if he is worthy of receiving an answered prayer. These are all destructive ego reactions. A fake person is praying to a fake god; and as a result, he gets fake answers and responses. Man's imagination also houses all his beliefs about life. Most of these beliefs are erroneous and negative. This is why he is so neurotic. His mind is a house of horrors causing him to be afraid of just about everything and everyone. His mind is a jumbled up cluster of fears, negativity, noise, and nonsense that he mistakes as being reality. The reason why he believes it to be reality is because his ego (the fake person) is inclusive in the cluster. The ego is right there with the nonsense; therefore, it accepts the nonsense as being real. It cannot be otherwise since it too is fake. These negative beliefs and ideas are working against him: cancelling out his prayers. This is the way that it must be. Since the ego is fake, then it has to deceive you in whatever way it can so that you won't see that it isn't real. Every now and then, by the law of averages, a man may come into a sum of money, avoid an accident, have a physical illness clear up, or something of that nature; he will then proudly announce how the Lord came through for him and delivered him from his troubles. This will be his constant testimony until the law of averages causes some other fortunate event to take place in his life, but his so called victories are too few and far between. What he won't testify to are the countless prayers that have gone unanswered. He won't mention the crying and desperate pleas for help that were too often ignored. What he will do, however, is say that his unanswered prayers were not in God's will: which, by the way, is a lie. This is how he compensates for his misery. His ego tells him that God wants him to remain miserable; God doesn't want you to have this particular victory or that special blessing. You should be ashamed to have such selfish or self centered prayers when there are so many others that are less fortunate, is another ego trick that a man falls for. In a nutshell, God's will is that you should "have life and have it more abundantly." The ego is crafty. It has no choice but to fool the man, if it were to do otherwise, then the man would develop a real relationship with God resulting in the dissolution of the ego. The ego is afraid of destruction. It does not want to die, so it keeps itself alive by fooling, thwarting, or in some cases, mentally destroying the actual man. The ego must keep the man in a miserable state in order to keep its imaginary existence in tact. The Real Man is not afraid of anything whatsoever. The ego is afraid of all. A man does not fear to die. His ego fears death. It has the man fooled into believing that he is afraid to come to the end of his life, his thoughts, and his body, but the ego is the thing doing the fearing, not the man. By keeping man afraid, the ego keeps itself from dying. Man does not know that his imagination runs his life. He does not know that he has an imaginary god. He does not know that he is sabotaging himself this way from within. His unawareness is his only problem. Man is hypnotized or spiritually asleep and must wake up.

Man must wake up.

The only way for a man to wake up is to realize what is happening to him. In order to realize what is happening he has to see it. He has to acknowledge that what is happening to him is not beneficial or necessary. He has to stop justifying the nonsense, drama and negativity in order to see what a mess he is in. He must accept responsibility for the mess he is in and not blame anyone or anything: not his parents, teachers, brothers, sisters, friends, the devil, God, or even himself. He must stop letting himself off the hook by saying it is or isn't God's will. By giving himself no excuses for his frazzled mental life, the process of ego destruction begins, and like it says in the Bible; he begins to be transformed by the renewing of his mind.

Rebirth: mind takes its rightful and secondary place while spirit is restored to its original position of authority and a man's awareness now habitually resides outside of his mind.

Are you out of your mind?

You've heard that question before haven't you? Or you may have heard the expression, "you must be out of your mind." Someone probably said it to you out of anger or surprise when you did or said something that they didn't like or thought was stupid. You may have felt insulted and your feelings were hurt. If you felt hurt or offended by the expression, then the answer is "no." You were not out of your mind. You were very much inside of your mind: self absorbed and self centered. You made yourself the center of the Universe, and your feelings were hurt because you got knocked off your pedestal. The other person that hurled the insult at you is the center of the Universe in his mind, and he dethroned you. After which, if you returned the insult, you reclaimed your title by dethroning him. So it goes, back and forth, you argue and fight until exhausted. The conflict always ends in a stalemate; even if you got the last word and think that you've won, nobody truly wins. As far as you are concerned, you are still the center of your own personal universe, and in his mind, he is still the center of his own personal universe. The problem is that you both are unaware people. There is only One Universe and neither of you are truly the center. You both are living in delusion, and if you were truly "out of your mind," as the other person had said you where, then you would've answered in a calm way with a simple "yes, I am out of my mind" without any angry flare ups or retorts, and you would've left it at that. To be out of your mind does not mean that you are crazy; quite the opposite, to be out of your mind is sanity.

Book I. Reflections:

1. Spiritual growth is possible through self observation.
2. Impartial self observation is to consciously see or become aware of everything that goes on inside and outside of yourself.
3. Spiritual growth is achieved through the de-conditioning and dehypnotizing of the mind.
4. You have a dual personality. There is a Real You that is directly connected to God and a false you that is the coveted ego.
5. The Real Self must be contacted and the false self must be dismissed.
6. Knowing that God is real is possible only through first seeing that the ego is fake.
7. A man must wake up first by realizing what has happened to him. He must see that the ego has taken over and ruined his life.
8. Being out of your mind equates to sanity.

Book II

The Only Issue You Have: A Fake ID

You've heard stories about people impersonating others or misrepresenting themselves by way of fake id's. The only issue you have is a primary fear. That primary fear is the fear of death: the death of your fake id. Whether you know it or not, you fear the end of your fake id. Yes, you are a fake. You have a fake id. It's called an "ego." You have been hypnotized over the years into believing that you are something or someone that you are not. You may be a doctor, lawyer, minister, or whatever; however, these are only labels for outward identification. The issue is that you've mentally internalized the labels and created a false persona. Proof of this fake id is the actual hypnotized or negatively conditioned mind. If you are a doctor and someone calls you a "quack." You may react with anger because of the conditioned mind. The mind is conditioned to believe in the power and reality of the label as opposed to just being a doctor without identifying with the title. Identifying with the label is what causes mental and emotional vulnerability. If the label is disputed or insulted, then the feelings get hurt.

The "fear of death" mentioned above is not about physical death. It is a psychological death; it is the ego fearing that its imaginary existence may come to an end. The doctor reacts with hurtful emotions when called a quack because he has an illusion in his mind of being a good doctor. This illusion is egotistical (a self opinion of and belief about his character), but he is unaware of this. He may think that it is truth because in the past he's been told by others that he is good or perhaps he's even won awards, but yet and still, it is an opinion that he mentally clings to, and he fails to understand that others may not agree with it. When insulted, the insult is viewed as an attack. The attack is seen by the ego as an attempt to take away the self imposed belief that it is a good doctor. This means that it thinks a part of itself is being taken away. It believes it is being killed, so it defends itself by getting upset.

Most humans spend their days being driven, distracted, or tortured by their minds and erroneous thought processes. Their minds are on automatic pilot in a negative way and constantly burning up valuable energy that could be used for constructive or creative purposes. These stressful and negative thought processes rob them of the very vitality and spirituality they seek and takes away their focus, thereby causing procrastination which develops into boredom that gives birth to a sinister mindset that "life is passing me by." Other mindsets just like this are also taking place simultaneously: mindsets like, "what's the use," "nobody really cares," or "it's hopeless," are only a few.

Peace of mind isn't something that you strive to achieve. It is something that is already built into your mindset by nature. Because of your fake id, you have the illusion that negativity is a built in and permanent part of you. The average human being is a frightened, timid, and fearful person. The average person is a small child trapped in an adult body. Some may appear to be braver than others, but don't you believe it. They are just as fake. A true spiritual person is a very rare and unafraid human being, but he does exist. He is probably one in ten million. People go through all kinds of tortuous processes in an effort be a spiritual person. Some even starve themselves; some practice meditation, black or white magic and pray; some even pray with snakes or breathe in special ways, and do special (physical) exercises. Whether any of these processes work or not, I cannot say, but I can say that they are not necessary. You may be thinking, "Wait a minute, how can prayer not be necessary? Don't worry, that will be touched upon later. You only need two tools in order to cure yourself. Those tools are natural God given abilities called "awareness and self honesty." Used correctly, awareness and self honesty will not only dissolve your negative and fearful mindset, but will put you in a position to where you will never have to believe anything about God and His agenda. You will know at all times what God wants and requires of you and have the will and enthusiasm to carry out His guidance. You won't have to think about a thing. You won't be afraid to carry out His instructions. You won't be concerned with what others think. You will know exactly what to do and when to do it. Another way that people try to become more spiritual is with the use of positive thinking. In most cases this method not only results in failure, but when failure occurs (by the way failure is an illusion, but you don't realize that yet) it leaves the individual in a worse state of mind by solidifying other mindsets like, "What's the use of trying, nothing will change." This can turn into such a vicious cycle and downward spiral that in the worse case scenarios will lead an individual to the brink of insanity, or he may develop conditions like bad tempers, depression, loneliness, anxiety, phobias, or even dementia which is another word for insanity. As a matter of fact, it's all insanity. I truly believe that insanity and dementia are defense mechanisms that an individual has employed in order to escape from a world that has frightened them to the point of no return. No; positive thinking is not the answer. Awareness is. You must become aware of your negative thought processes and once you do that, you must use self honesty to help with the fake id's dissolution process. Yes, the ego (fake id) can be dissolved leaving you with blissful peace of mind.

Most people may think that they are already aware of their negative minds and thoughts, but the truth is that they are self absorbed in their negative mind. Awareness is not the same as self absorption. Also, having an intellectual or mental knowing of something isn't the same thing as being aware. Awareness is a spiritual attribute; it isn't mental at all. You can read a book about bald eagles and gain intellectual knowledge, but will never be aware of what the bird is truly about until you observe it: big difference. Awareness dwells outside of the negative mind even while looking at the mental processes. It's not in the mind at all.

Right now your awareness, being, or spirit dwells via the imagination within your mind instead of in outside reality or the present moment, and this is why you are so fearful and negative. This is what perpetuates the ego's existence in your mind.

Your mind houses all kind of crazy and ridiculous beliefs, and your awareness is fully immersed in all of that nonsense. No wonder you're so afraid. Your present time awareness or spirit has been replaced by your mind's terrifying imagination. You have traded your fearless spirit for the "haunted house" of your mind, and that is why you have a fake id. All your beliefs and ideas about yourself have taken over your life in an evil way.

You live your life by way of phony and erroneous beliefs which institute a negative non stop imaginary world that you can't escape. Be honest; isn't your mind always racing and rambling? You believe that these phony beliefs and useless ideas housed by your mind are your identity.

This belief in the negative imaginary cluster of phony ideas is what the ego (fake id) is; this false identity even comes across as being a real entity. Your current beliefs about yourself whether positive or negative have been animated by your inverted awareness.

Inverted awareness means that your center of attention and perception is clouded over by your mind's negative neurotic racing. It should be grounded in the "present moment," the "here and now." You can begin to reverse the process. You can turn your awareness right side up or inside out and put your mind in its proper place thereby curing all of your mental and even some physical ills. You, by taking baby steps at first, can with persistence regain your victorious spiritual identity, and in this state, you won't even be concerned about an identity. You will know who you are at all times without even having to think about who you are.

Awareness vs. Absorption:

Knowing the difference between self awareness and self absorption is an ultimate aim of spiritology and the one and only key to spiritual rebirth. This is the crux of the matter if you are to be successful in spiritual growth. Awareness is a calm seeing of your mental state whereas absorption is being sucked into and hypnotized by your imagination all the while believing that you are aware. With awareness, negative emotions have no effect on you and can do no harm, but absorption not only carries you away to an inner fantasy land or horror house, but causes you to behave impulsively, mechanically, and destructively. With awareness, you preserve and increase inner strength and physical energy; with absorption, you drain inner strength and physical energy. With practice, you will be able to decipher the difference between the two and thereby hasten your spiritual growth. You must see the difference.

Here is an astonishing fact, that if accepted, could be the greatest revelation of your life and bring with it the pleasant and sunny spiritual skies that you were meant to dwell up under.

You are scared of yourself:

Are you afraid to face your fears? You shouldn't be. It's easier than you think. What is fear? Fear is a feeling that is manufactured based upon a thought about yourself, the world, or your life. If fears are only feelings generated from thoughts, then you are afraid of your own thoughts. Your thoughts are inside of you; they are a part of your psyche. Your psyche is a part of you. It is the thought about the situation that is producing the terror not the outside circumstance. Since your thoughts are within you (a part of you), then to be afraid of your thoughts is to be afraid of yourself. Imagine that! You are scared of yourself: your false self! This translates to the ego being afraid of itself. Only the ego can be irrationally afraid, and all irrational fear is ego generated. Does that sound silly? Well, here is something even more astounding than that. To be afraid of yourself, translates to being afraid of life. You may say, "How can that be? If I was afraid of life, then I'd want out and would've killed myself by now. Don't jump the gun too fast because you are also afraid of death. Remember? The ego also fears its death.

The fear of life includes being afraid of everyone and everything in life; that also includes the fear of death. Yes, the ego also fears (physical) death. Since death is a transition in life then it is a part of life, but many mistakenly believe that death is the opposite of life. Life is Life, and Life is Eternal. Life has no equal or opposite because God is Life. No one can really explain what Life is. Death has nothing to do with Life but is encompassed by Life, so therefore death is not the opposite of Life but is a part of the cycle of Life. Birth (the animation of a physical body) is the opposite of death (the de-animation of a physical body), and like death, birth is a part of the cycle of Life. Birth is a transition or gateway to this earthly plane, and death is a gateway to another realm. You fear death because you are uncertain to what is on the other side, and you're not sure what you're getting into. It is basically a fear of the unknown and fear of change. You don't fear death. Your false ego self fears death (the death of itself). Since your Real Self (the personality beyond the ego) is one with God, then by its very nature, it cannot fear anything, and that includes death. How can God be afraid of anything? God has no fear whatsoever. God is Life and Life is eternal. God cannot die; therefore, God cannot be afraid of death. Only physical bodies are temporal. These bodies die and are reborn. Look at your own physical body. Depending upon how old you are, your body has died and been reborn multiple times. This is happening on a cellular level. Think about it. Science has already proven that cells are constantly dying and being reborn. You can even see this for yourself, as when a wound heals or your skin peels. The flesh replaces and replenishes itself. Yes, the flesh was lost, but was either reborn or recreated. You know that it happened, but you probably didn't fret over it because the destroyed flesh came back like you knew it would. All the while, nothing happened to your Life. Your Life remained constant and eternally secure in God, as it is. Science has proven that every cell in your entire body has been replaced and is continuously being replaced at this very moment. The flesh dies but not the life. Since you have no fear of death on the cellular level, then there is no need to fear it on a larger level. When your full physical body dies, your Life will remain as constant as it does on the cellular level of death, and just like on the cellular level, you will be totally reborn (resurrected as Christ taught). As you begin to dissolve the ego, this insight comes by gradual revelation.

More on fear:

Fear is emotional pain, and emotional pain is fear. They are synonymous or one and the same, and your mind is fully occupied with both. Just about everything you do or say is from the ego and is therefore fear based whether you know it or not. You will at some point have to realize this fact if you want to achieve self healing. Just like the body, the mind is designed by God to be a self healing mechanism. You really don't need to do anything to it; you just let it happen.

Your mind houses all kinds of pain and fear that are mostly attached to distant and sometimes recent memories or traumatic experiences. You are even afraid of this pent up fear and trauma because you are afraid of anything that you perceive will ignite the fear and trauma and bring it to the surface of your mind. Some people go through great and ridiculous measures to avoid the feeling of being afraid. They get afraid of the possibility of being afraid so out of fear, they attempt to avoid fear;

how about that? You are afraid of your fears. Since you are afraid of your fears and pain, your mind masks the fear and pain so that you can better cope with it. One way it copes and masks fear is by using labels to justify your fear. This labeling keeps fear in tact and the justification prevents healing: labels like hostility, depression, loneliness, even false excitement. A hostile man may justify his hostility by believing that it keeps people afraid and respectful of him and therefore provides him with a sense of power. All the other negative labels and emotions are also being justified in some way. For whatever reason the man thinks that the negative feelings are necessary to his psychological survival and overall well being. He believes that he needs his negativity. These labels are all forms of the one fear that is the entire composition of the ego. It masks fear because it knows that you don't like pain, so it calls pain something else like "depression" so that it can fool you into believing that it is ok to suffer; at the same time the ego knows that you don't want to get rid of it either because you've identified with it so you think it is the real you, and to get rid of it would mean no more you. Not true!

Your mind is always trying to push pain up from your subconscious depths to the surface so that the pain can be expelled. It sometimes uses outside stimuli to call up the fear to be dealt with. This is the real reason why you may react to outer circumstances with fear, anger, depression, or some other fear based emotion. Yep, your mind is trying to heal itself, but in the past, you may not have known that your mind was trying to do this, so you deal with it in the wrong way. You listen to your ego which tells you to justify your negative state, and by doing so, you feed the negative emotion and intensify it while simultaneously keeping the ego self alive. For instance, a man has a bad temper, and his ego tells him, "It keeps people afraid of you and is necessary for you to be respected. It gives you power over others because they fear you." Or a depressed man's ego may say, "Your wife just left you. You're supposed to be depressed." Here is the biggest egotistical lie of them all. Your ego says, "Its ok." This is what egotistical people share amongst themselves. One sees another hurting and says, "Its ok. You have every right to feel this way." You have the right to be upset, scared, depressed, and annoyed. Don't listen to the lies! Listen to God! God says, "Don't listen to those unaware people. They don't know what they're talking about. Don't listen to your ego! Listen to me for a change! Listen to Me and be victorious!" The consolations, whining, and crying are all ego based and destructive. If you really think about these emotions, you will eventually conclude that they are all forms of fear or pain, and you will stop labeling and giving diversity to fear and pain. You will stop seeing fear as an entity of multiplicity and view it for what it really is: a painful but imaginary self that thinks it is separate from God. There is no depression or anger; there is only the feeling of fear that the ego has fooled you into believing is something else, and since it is something else, I can justify it and tell myself that is it ok to be miserable. Think about it. If you were to start examining your anger or depression or any other negative state, then you would realize that it is a painful state. You'd then conclude that pain isn't beneficial. This process would start to unravel the puzzle that is the ego; so tell yourself the truth about your condition, and you will eventually come to the conclusion that you are not depressed or angry, but afraid. You would then reason that it doesn't make sense to be afraid of this situation or that person; and the ego would relinquish its hold on you. Telling yourself the truth is only the beginning. You must also accept the truth. Acceptance is what allows truth to penetrate your psyche, and the newly accepted truth begins its clearing processes and starts to renew your mind.

Acceptance can be a little tricky at first. Why? Because all your life you have been living by way of ego acceptance. What this means is that you hear some empowering knowledge. It is mentally taken in by your ego and stored as dormant memorized data, whereas if it was taken in by way of conscious acceptance, it would be installed as an empowering belief that gives you the fearless audacity to act it out and implement it in full measure. You are processing useful knowledge by way of egotism as opposed to spiritual awareness. This is why people (especially Christians) dish out inspiring quotes, claim how blessed they are, but continue on in mental misery. You will be given the way to achieve awareness during the course of this book.

Think about an intense fear that you may have. The fear may be labeled as some kind of phobia. In the moment, you think that you are afraid of an outside circumstance like heights or public speaking, but you are not. You are afraid of the thought about the situation. Your mind uses the circumstance as a catalyst to bring the fear to the surface so that you can observe it, but you don't examine it; instead, you become mentally absorbed, and continue to be afraid of the thought. If you were to take the away the thought about the height or the audience, the circumstance would still be the same but the phobia would not exist. It is the erroneous thought that is causing the mayhem. Proof from the flip side: sometimes the situation may not even be in the present moment: not happening yet. I may have to give a speech tomorrow or a week from now, but if I fear pubic speaking, then the fear wells up from within at this very moment even though nothing is going on. Fear only penetrates the situation from thoughts about what may happen. Even if the circumstance is happening in the present moment, the fear is always about what may happen (in the future). Put a person that is scared of heights on a rollercoaster. If he is able to shift his focus to present moment and the rollercoaster itself, then fear would be totally absent; he would enjoy the ride; if he starts to think about the possibility of falling, then he is thinking about something that hasn't happened and getting scared of a perceived possibility. This is what the ego needs to survive: irrational thoughts based upon the past or future. Irrational thought is its food and nourishment. Shift your awareness to the present moment; the ego and its accompanying fear vanishes! Try it.

Again, the issue is that you don't recognize what your mind is trying to do when it pushes up the fear, so you either wallow in the hurtful emotion, get absorbed in the negative mental pictures, or you suppress it all. These are all unhealthy actions, and suppression by far is the worst thing you can do. Next time you encounter a fearful situation, look at the fear. Don't try to suppress or justify it. Just let it be there and look at it. Be aware of it and present with it. Watch (be aware of) how your body goes through its reactions: sweaty palms, shaky knees, etc. Watch whatever frantic or panicky thoughts that arise. Watch everything that goes on: inside and out. This is the way of getting rid of fear. Get rid of the fear of your thoughts and presto! You are spiritually reborn!

Begin to face your fear on a daily basis; here is the way to do so, use the power of your awareness to start catching yourself in the middle of fear. Your only purpose is to observe it. It is not necessary that you try and use your intellect to examine, analyze, or decipher anything, just look (impartially) at the fear and leave it at that. This will produce incredible results; make it a habit of going around situations that you fear in an effort to observe the fear. Start with minor fears first.

One last tidbit on fear:

The key to facing fear is to face (impartially observe) the fear itself (face the feeling of fear not the outside circumstance).

Positive Thinking:

The thing about positive thinking is that it has an opposite which is negative thinking. You have to put forth an effort to work at it, and if you are trying to do it, then you are simultaneously thinking negative. Because the trying is a struggle in an of itself and mental struggle is always a negative thing. If you say to yourself, "I am strong in the Lord." Your sinister subconscious will send forth the negative troops and say something like, "Well, if you are so strong, then why did you let so and so push you around yesterday?" Then the other may come back, "Well, I didn't want to be rude in front of everybody." Now comes the opposition, "What does that matter? You know that you are fed up with this person and wanted to take a stand." The battle continues back and forth. You think positive and then shoot yourself down with a negative thought. Even before you start the positive thought, you can see the negative waiting in ambush. This is what the fake id is all about and you can't change it. You can dissolve it however with awareness. Awareness is not a thinking process; it is pure observation and perception without thinking. It is knowing as opposed to thinking. It is anchored in the present moment that has no worries or concerns. The thought processes have ceased. Yes, it is possible to still your mind. There is a part of you that is not mental or physical: it is your awareness, being, or spirit. It is the entity that you perceive inside your head that is peeking out at the world through the eyeballs. Just by watching everything inside and outside of you, without thinking about what you see, you can become a true, "Child of God," positive thinking is not necessary, but will be come automatic just as negative thinking is now automatic once you free yourself of the fake id. Perhaps the terminology should be practical or constructive thinking instead of positive thinking.

The Amplified Bible, book of Proverbs 20:27 says, "The spirit of man (that factor in human personality which proceeds immediately from God) is the lamp of the Lord, searching all his innermost parts." The factor in human personality that proceeds immediately from God is the Real You; it is your Spirit. It is the detached observer.

As you go through your day, notice how many times you get afraid. Just notice and leave it at that. Don't beat yourself up about it. Just notice. Don't try to make excuses for your fear; just impartially observe. Naturally, a negative conditioned mind will try to put its two cents in to justify or make excuses by saying something like, "this is a dog eat dog world, who wouldn't be afraid?" If that happens, don't worry about it. Observing the way your mind makes excuses and justifications is an excellent starting point. It will happen very frequently in the beginning, but with diligence, it will happen less and less until you are able to notice without justifying and leave it at that. Also, don't try to suppress; let yourself be afraid so that you can observe the feeling.

Your fake id or false sense of self is who you think you are at the moment. You have identified with so many labels in your lifetime that these labels have combined into one big cluster of negative and fearful nonsense, and have come to life (imaginary life) and set themselves up as a seemingly real person within your mind. Your labels about yourself have given you a sense of separation from God and life. You even have labels from when you where a small child that you've never released. Now you know why in certain situations, a 50 year old acts like a 5 year old. Something in the environment triggered a response and as a defense mechanism the person acted like a child because he or she knew no better. You were never taught how to behave in a mature manor or release these childish labels and defense mechanisms, so they've become buried in your psyche and to this day still affect your behavior. Yes, even the labels from when you were an infant can be wreaking havoc in your life at this very moment. Think about the labels you may have. I am mother or father. I am a doctor or lawyer. I am a student. I am a Christian. I am a winner or loser. I am a good man or woman. I am unemployed. I am overworked and underpaid. The list goes on. What about the labels that you still carry from your childhood? I am just a baby. Here are some of the author's labels that had to be overcome from childhood because unaware people dished out these labels for the purpose of control. I am lazy and trifling. I am a sorry person. I am sickly. I am hardheaded. I am scary. What about the horror movies and fairy tales you saw as a child that you've accepted as reality; they too are affecting your current adult behavior. You may think that you have an endless host of fears and don't know why: like fear of the dark and fear of commitment. There are certainly many more, but you get the point. Stop believing that you have so many fears and see that you have one false sense of self (an ego). Restored mental health will be the result.

Book II. Reflections:

1. The only issue you have is the ego and its fearful nature.
2. Positive thinking won't solve anything, but awareness will cure everything.
3. Awareness is a calm seeing of your mental state. Absorption means to be sucked into and carried away by your mental state.
4. Learn the difference between self awareness and self absorption.
5. The only fear that really plagues your mind is the ego's fear of its own destruction.
6. Fear and emotional pain are one and the same.
7. Whenever a negative state pops up, realize that it's your mind trying to heal you and become aware of the negativity.
8. Tell yourself the truth about fear on a consistent basis, and it will eventually go away.
9. Positive thinking isn't something you should have to work at.
10. Unemotionally pay attention to how often you get scared.

Book III

In the beginning:

When you were born, you received your very first label: boy or girl. Then your second label, your name, came along. For a while you were innocent and did not internalize these labels. But all of the unaware people around you started the process of hypnotizing you, causing you to personalize these labels instead of using them as a form of outward identification. You were taught or hypnotized into believing that you and these labels are one and the same. If you are a girl, you were told, "You are a girl, and girls are this or girls should act like that." You were taught and coerced to act out a phony role as opposed to simply being what you truly are. From your infancy until now, you started and kept on adding more labels; you became very skilled at doing this, and the labeling never stopped. Like a snowball rolling down hill, over the years, this cluster labels that make up your false id attached themselves to each other and grew bigger and bigger; now you call yourself everything under the sun; the very same thing also happened to just about all other people; everyone else has their own set of labels; the conclusion reached is that we are separated from each other and separated from God. Labels have one function, and that is for worldly identification. Labels are useful when having to communicate with each other, but to believe in and internalize (emotionalize) these labels is to set up a false id which in turn causes division and conflict between you and your fellow

49

man. These labels or your fake id causes division between you and God and this is why you are scared, angry, depressed, bored, resentful, guilt ridden, and any other negative state that you can think of. It is because of these labels that you swing from happiness to depression or excitement in one moment and boredom in the next. Because of these internalized labels, you believe that your happiness and security depend on worldly things that are here one day and gone the next: things like money, a new car or home, a spouse, a church home, a flourishing career, etc...

You have no real sense of security and you never will until you are able to put these labels in their proper place psychologically. Until you put these labels in their correct mental position, you can never truly know, commune with, walk with, worship, or even pray to God. God alone is happiness and security; God needs nothing outside of Himself to exist; many people are claiming that they are secure in God but fool themselves because at other times they will say, "It's hopeless. Things will never change, but in the afterlife it will be better. I'll never accomplish my goals. The world is out to get me. People just don't understand me. I'm not worried because God knows my heart. Tomorrow things will be better." The previous statements are not faith based which is why tomorrow is usually a repeat of what an individual is experiencing today. Faith alone is the key, hope is useless. Why? Because hope carries with it a vague sense of doubt and unnecessary concern. Hope carries with it false confidence and worry.

Faith is real. It is beyond confidence. It is beyond belief. Faith is knowing. There is a difference between believing and knowing. A belief could be wrong. Knowing is always correct. Believing takes effort and is always riddled with uncertainty. Knowing takes no effort and is rock solid faith. A friend can describe the inside of his new home to you. You may believe him, but you don't really have an accurate accounting based upon your mind's interpretation of his words. He may have misrepresented something or your own mind may have envisioned something totally unlike what he told you. One day you go to visit. You look at the home for yourself and become aware of what it really is like. Now you know without having to believe. This is how the vast of humanity's relationship with God is. They've been told about God, read about God, but have never met God. They now attempt to believe without knowing and their lives prove it. Get rid of the ego/false self and there is God waiting for you with open arms.

Put First thing first:

A climber can only conquer one mountain at a time. Common sense dictates this fact to you. You may think that you are a multitasker, but in reality, in the moment, you can only perform one task. The issue with having too many irons in the fire is that eventually something gets placed on a back burner; later, you may recall this task and bring it to the foreground to work on, but if you haven't finished the task you were originally working on, you loose momentum on the original task and delay its completion. If you are a creature of habit, like most people are, then it's highly likely that the task that has now been pulled off the back burner will take a back seat to a third task or the original task that are now on the back burners. The multitasking illusion is why so many people fail to accomplish anything, especially spiritual growth. They spend so much time and energy with worldly affairs and attempt to relate to God whenever their busy schedules allow it. As far as multitasking goes, even if they do succeed and get multiple tasks done, it takes a much longer time to accomplish than if they had decided to prioritize the tasks and complete them one at a time. If you start on a task and gain momentum, then the momentum continues to increase and you finish in a faster amount of time because the momentum is accompanied with the power of your increasing focus. If you start a task and stop in order to start another, then both momentum and focus are lost on the original task and now you are faced with an extra task of becoming focused and building momentum on this new task you've started. Frustration is sure to set in and if your mind is racing with too many items to focus on then it's highly likely that the mental processes will falter or even shut down; procrastination will intervene and nothing will get done. Prioritize what is most important for you by making a list and doing one thing at a time. As Christ alluded to, your main priority should be seeking the Kingdom (dissolving the fake id) and afterwards everything else shall be added unto you. Make the seeking of the Kingdom your first and foremost priority. Think about it. How silly would it be if a climber had 3 mountains to climb, and midway up the first one, he decided to descend so that he can start climbing the second? He climbs the second one a bit and then again decides to go back to the ground in order to climb the third. You'd probably think to yourself, "That is a wacky climber. He'll never make it to the top of any of those mountains using that type of methodology," but this is how a lot of people handle their day to day activities and responsibilities. Put first thing first: seek the Kingdom.

Taking the Next Step:

If you have tried the path of spiritual growth before, then it is probable that you are familiar with this concept: "Taking the next step." In theory, on the spiritual path, you should never get ahead of yourself. The reason why so many people fall off the path is because they lack patience. They try to think ahead to the distant future and use their imaginations in an attempt to see what real enlightenment is or what it will be like. Then they try to mentally make it happen. Since enlightenment is outside of the mind and mental processes, that makes any mental attempt futile. The imagination (ego) futilely paints all sort of weird and fantastic (false) pictures of what the Kingdom is like which frustrates the seeker's efforts. This frustration leads to a sense of hopelessness, and the seeker gives up. You are used to using your mind this way on the material plane, and that is fine. Using your mind to plan for the material is practical and is what your mind was meant to do; you are at work and you know that you have several items to contend with, so you use your mind for futuristic thinking as follows: get off at 3 in order to beat traffic to get to baby sitter's by 4:30 in order to make it home by 5 so that dinner can be served at 6. Futuristic thinking is only meant to plan on the material level; keep this in mind. Always remember to see where you are and take the next step with out worrying about the step after. Once you take the next step, and see where you are, then the step that follows will become obvious to you; you can then move forward once again. This is how the spiritual path works; take one step at a time without thinking ahead and you will enter the Kingdom; remember, Christ said, "Take no thought for tomorrow."

A side thought about the next step:

It is about confusion. There will be times when you are utterly confused about what the next step is. Your mind will race and you will feel helpless and lost. Fear will kick in and you will start the ego thinking of, "Gee, what's the use? I'm lost and confused; how can I take the next step when all I can see is a thick fog of confusion?" Here is the good news. I will give you the next step. Whenever you are in this predicament (and this one can go on seemingly forever), the next step is to do absolutely nothing! Nothing? But how can it be? I gotta do something you say (the ego says). How can I move forward by doing nothing? Ahh... Glad you asked. In the material world, if you walk from your house to the grocery store to purchase some milk, you take one step at a time until you get to the market, then you find the isle where the milk is, then to the check out counter and you pay; afterwards, you walk back home; this is the way the material plane works; if you are confused upon the whereabouts of the store, then there is nothing you can do until you received some kind of directions to the store; right? So it is with confusion on the spiritual path, if you are confused, how can you know what the next step is? Confusion means that a situation is not clear, and because of its very nature, there is nothing you can do until you are no longer confused; if there is nothing you can do, then that is exactly what you should do; absolutely nothing. By doing nothing, you are doing something which is still forward progress because you are doing the only thing you can do: nothing. Rest in the confusion and use the power of impartial self observation, to look at the confusion. By resting in it and watching it, you are taking the next step, and then the next, and then the next, and although it may appear that you are stagnant, you are in reality moving forward (growing) so don't ever fret over confusion. At some point it will clear up, and whatever the next step is after that, will be revealed for you to take; you will get to the store get your goods and make it back home on the spiritual path as well.

God's grace:

Not by your own mind power or will power or even physical power, but only by God's Grace will your life unfold as it should. Religious folk constantly proclaim how they live by the Grace of God when nothing could be further from the Truth. The sad evidence of their lifestyles prove that they don't. Forget about what they tell you and look how they live. This in and of itself is a tremendous challenge. We've conditioned ourselves to listen to and put our trust in each other's empty words. We insist that we know how action speaks louder than words, but we always fall back into putting our trust into the words. Folks that loudly proclaim to live by Grace live just like everyone else; they try to force or will life to happen which is not how it works. Life can only be lived; it cannot be forced, and by keeping this spiritual fact in mind, you are well on the way to entering the Grace of God. By forcing life or trying to will life, the fruit of frustration will be the ultimate result. Whatever seeds you sow, you reap the same harvest. Over a lifetime of trying to command life, lets say 70 or 80 years, an individual becomes bitter with life, regretful over life, and even more fearful of life. Even if they did get the money, fame, power, or whatever they wanted, it was probably a gruesome struggle, and the result still turned out to be mental anguish in spite of the worldly gain. The author believes that people who suffer from dementia, senility, or other similar mental conditions have led such a lifetime of fear and frustration that their minds couldn't handle reality anymore, so it devised a method of escape. They became a child again or lost whatever rationality they had, and as some people put it, "they went crazy." Think about how often you've tried to will life to happen and recall the result of what actually happened. Compare the way a plan unfolded in your mind with the way it happened in real life. Did other people involved do or say what you thought they should? Did the event go exactly as you had planned it in your head? If not, did you get frustrated, upset, or disappointed? Probably so, and if you want to look forward to a lifetime of upsets and frustrations, then trying to will things to happen by your own mind power will ensure that you get it. You want to live by God's Grace, and again, a simple way to do it is like this. Don't try to change your methodology. Do the same technique as in the upcoming "Prayer is not necessary" segment. Remember, self awareness blossoms via self observation which is the key to freedom and victory.

God's Grace: small examples:

Here are a couple of small examples of God's grace. A couple of days ago, I was walking down the street in the downtown area where I work. I had decided to go off property for lunch. At the time, the city was doing repairs on the street. As the big back hoe was pounding away at the loose pavement it stirred up a lot of dust. Coincidentally, it was very windy that day and the dust was blowing in my direction. Anticipating the worst, I started squinting my eyes to prevent dust from blowing into them; however, dust inevitably blew into them. The grit of the dust was very painful, and my eyes started to sting. Once I got out of the range of the blowing dust, a miraculous thing happened. It is a miracle that has happened to me many times before, but I have always taken it for granted. My eyes started to tear up and became very watery. In a matter of seconds, the water washed all of the dust out of my eyes and a soothing feeling came over my eyeballs during the process. I blinked my eyes very hard several times, and finally, I could feel that all the dust had been washed away. At that point, the tears stopped flowing. I thought to myself, "Wow, there was an immediate need for cleansing and relief and the need was fulfilled without me having to do anything or ask for it." The very next day, I was at work, and again, it was lunchtime. It dawned on me that I didn't have any cash, and I knew that my checking account was very low, so I didn't want to take the chance on using it and incurring an overdraft fee. I also didn't want to go online and transfer money out of my savings. The thought of skipping lunch all together crossed my mind, but I was hungry. I don't remember exactly what happened after that because something else had gotten my attention, and I had to tend to it. In the course of doing so, I had to take a trip to the purchasing department. Once I got there, the purchasing manager said to me, "hey we got some pizza here, if you want some, feel free to help yourself." Again, I thought to myself, "Another example of God's grace." Afterwards, I proceeded to eat pizza. These are examples of God's Grace in a nutshell. How many have you experienced today? Recognize and stop taking them for granted. This is how you make way for the larger miracles to occur, although in the Eyes of God, the miracle of parting the red sea is no larger or smaller than the miracle

of tears washing dust out of the eyes. It is your
level of faith that prompts the activation.

Grace just happened. I didn't will it to happen or
try to force it to happen; it just happened. It
happened because there was a need and a
recognition of the need, and that is all there was to
it. I have had countless small miracles like this
during my lifetime. These are the so called minor
examples. The Bible and other religious books also
teach that for God, the so called large miracles are
just as easy to perform as the so called small ones.
They are both the same in the eyes of God. Again,
there was no willpower involved. The only 2
ingredients are the immediate need and the
recognition of the need. Leave it alone after that.
In other words see the need, then, let go and let
God. If you start to worry or try to mentally force
or determine or imagine how it should happen,
then you block the Grace and postpone your
miracle. I believe that if you are reading this, then
you know all about the so called "small" examples
of Grace. Did you recognize them as Grace or did
you take them for granted? I hope the former is
the case. Ok now, maybe you need a job or
something else on a so called "large" scale, but
your conditioned mind can't help itself. It worries
or tries to figure out how to make your large
miracle happen. Again, go ahead and allow your
mind to fret over your circumstance. Go ahead and
fret, but do so consciously. Fret, but don't become
absorbed in the fretting. Fret, but at the same time,
consciously see that you are fretting. Worry all you
want but know that you are worrying. Practice

every day this conscious seeing of your mental anguish. And again, I can't repeat it enough times. The anguish and worrying that blocks larger miracles will fade into nothingness and your miracles will burst through.

More on Miracles:

All things are possible to those that believeth (have faith). This is one of the most important messages that Christ delivered. I believe that anything is possible because of the simple fact that we, you and I, exist. A miracle like walking on water is amazing in and of itself, but to me, it doesn't hold a candle to the miracle of consciousness (being able to perceive and decipher colors and shapes, knowing the difference between and differentiating one human being from another, being able to feel, hear, and touch the surrounding environment); surely consciousness is the greatest of all miracles. If you think about it, without consciousness, life would be meaningless. Multiplying loaves of bread is an in credible feat, but yet and still it is a by-product of expanded consciousness. Miracles cannot be done without consciousness. The miracle worker is superior to the miracle.

I will use the word belief in a somewhat different context than the last section. In this section we aren't talking about blind belief. We're talking about the belief that comes with knowing once you have reunited your consciousness with God's.

I believe that it is possible to expand consciousness. The greater the range of consciousness, the easier it is to produce miracles. We move our bodies because of consciousness. Nerves and muscles work together at the prompting of consciousness. While it is true that there is an underlying Greater Intelligence (the Consciousness of God) controlling all the universal functions: the healing of a cut, the physical growth of a child, the in and out of the ocean tide, cellular reproduction, the planetary orbit of the solar system and other galaxies. I still believe that we, with our very own center of awareness, can wrought (Biblical like) miracles if we learn to expand our consciousness. Before awareness can be expanded, it must be uncovered by dissolving the ego, it must be brought up from the depths of the mind and imagination into the here and now, and when this is accomplished, we must discover a way to expand it beyond the physical body into our immediate physical environment: just like Christ's. Jesus performed miracles of such great magnitude (in the eyes of man) because of His expanded consciousness; He then went on to say, "These works that I do, you shall do even greater." The miracle of the dust washing out of my eyes happened because my consciousness expands at least to the parameters of my physical body. The miracle of Jesus multiplying the loaves of bread happened because of His vastly expanded consciousness; He was able to get food directly from the source of all things: God the Father. Because my consciousness expands to the borders of my physical body, the pizza came to me in a more scenic and familiar route. If I want to have a slice of bread to eat, I can only make it happen to the capacity that my consciousness allows or to the extent of which my consciousness has expanded. Since my consciousness only extends to encompass my physical body, then I must work with what I have. My consciousness commands my body, through the thought processes of my mind, to get up and get a slice of bread from the cupboard; but if my consciousness was extended in to the physical realm beyond my physical body (like Christ's was) then my mind is simultaneously extended as well, and I would be able to produce the bread in other ways: perhaps like the manna from Heaven that God delivered to Moses. Anything that the mind and awareness are connected to on a physical plane can be changed, moved, or manipulated. Once the mind is cleared, then the next step in spiritual elevation would be learning to extend consciousness past the immediate body and into the greater body that is the physical environment (body of God). Like Christ said, "According to your faith, it is done unto you."

Do the right thing:

Do the right thing internally and externally; this is the way to jumpstart God's grace. Giving up the struggle and doing the right thing is easier said than done. It's a pretty tall order and especially tough when dealing with people you don't like. The Bible teaches that outer acts of goodness or good deeds can't save a person. Only the Grace of God obtained by faith can save the individual. Think about karma on a grand scale when dealing with troublesome people. What comes around goes around, for every action there is a reaction, you reap what you sow. Most people will say that they believe in these statements or philosophies, but their lives tell a different tale. We all suffer from delusions of grandeur. We fantasize that doing the right thing is part of our mental make up and seldom realize that if it were, then our minds wouldn't be so tumultuous. The ego can never do the right thing simply because of its negative self-centered nature. Whether you believe it or not, the law of cause and effect is always operational, so you may as well align yourself with this law in order to make your life work. Thinking about karma on the grand scale means that you are doing the right thing in the moment for goodness sake. It may not be the popular thing to do in the moment and others may scorn you for thwarting their personal agendas. It may even seem like you are losing or missing out on something beneficial, but you must remember this. God is in control of the whole karma process, and the people that may seem to steal your reward in the moment for going against them are fleeting; those individuals come and go. God's laws are eternal, and your reward will present itself if you remain faithful. One immediate reward that never fails is that you move a little bit closer to God and away from egotism. Doing the right thing is part of the whole self rescue process; however, the inner mental reactions must correspond with the outer physical actions. Salvation cannot come if you give a derelict a dime in the outer world, but allow the inner world to become resentful of his begging. How many times have we given money to a homeless person and all the while these kinds of thoughts were swimming through the mind: "lazy bum, you need to get a job like everyone else." Grace comes from the actions of your inner world more so than the outer. There is a verse in the Bible that reads like this, and I paraphrase, "There are those who will claim, Lord I've done all of these good deeds in Your Name, fed the poor, healed the sick, etc...and the Lord responds, get away, I've never known you." And the reason being is that your inner world conflicts with the outer. Align the two worlds and you've got it made. Here is what you do. I'm sure that you encounter people that you don't like on a daily basis. Be nice to them no matter what. Keep in mind that being nice does not mean allowing someone to use, abuse, or take advantage of you. Listen to your common sense. All the while you are being nice, pay attention to how it eats at you on the inside. Watch the churning of your emotions. Let them toil all they want. Purposely go around people that you resent or don't like, if possible; you don't want to try this with volatile individuals of course, but just be near the negative ones. Maybe at lunch time in the break room, you can be near these people without having to deal with them. There are all kinds of ideal moments that you can use to let negative emotions pop up. All you need to do is consciously watch and be aware of the emotions. If someone says something crass, stupid, or mean, don't respond likewise. Give a polite nod or smile, and watch the confusion on their faces when they see that you are not drawn into their negative world. If it warrants a verbal response, then say something decent and respectful. Don't let stubborn pride get in the way. Stubborn pride will rear its ugly head and try to make you indignant. This is what you want, but not so that you can fire back on the rude person. You want this negative emotion of indignation to arise so that you can extirpate it once and for all by being aware that it's there; clear your mind this way by practicing doing the right thing, especially with people you don't like. Use these people and moments as golden opportunities to accelerate your spiritual growth.

Refuse to excuse:

Back yourself into a corner by refusing to excuse yourself. You may have heard that if you back a cat into a corner, it will be forced to fight its way out. And if it is forced to fight, it will win. You can use the same principle whenever a problem arises by refusing to excuse yourself by blaming others or by using some of the following cop outs. By refusing to blame anyone or anything, you force yourself into that corner thereby prompting the virtue of self reliance to kick in and fix your circumstances. There are many ways that the false self will attempt to cop out and in doing so, keep you in its treacherous clutches. Yes, your ego knows that if it can keep you attached to your problems and negative state of mind, then its existence is assured. Here are a four of the most notorious cop outs.

1. I am only human.

What makes us human? It is the ego that makes us human. Your ego is using you to make excuses for itself so that it can stay alive and continue to mess up your life. When are you going to decide to put an end to it? Don't wait too long because as the years go by, you will eventually come to a point where you will not want to eject your ego. At that point, you are officially insane. You've heard of or maybe you know people who suffer from dementia or like mental conditions. Plain and simple, that is insanity. Ditch this foolish justification.

2. I am not perfect.

Why are we not perfect? Again, it is because of the ego. Learn to see through its trickery. Learn to challenge it. Nothing but good can result. Continue to battle for yourself inwardly with the goal of reclaiming your Real Self kept in mind. Once your mind sees exactly what it is that you are trying to do, it will come to your aid. Intention is a very powerful weapon. Put it to work for you. Let go of this lame excuse.

has it been defined?

3. No one has the right to judge me.

People confuse telling the truth with being judgmental and vice versa. However, internally, we all know the difference. Whether or not it appears as being judgmental, it is crucial that you keep telling yourself the truth in order to escape from the human jungle created by ruthless egos. People frequently utter this phrase in a vain attempt to avoid the truth. Cease to employ this false reasoning. Didn't Christ say that the Father has given the rights to judgment to the son? Since we are joint heirs with Christ, who do you think has the right to judge you?

4. I'm still a babe in Christ.

There aren't many grown ups in Christ when it comes to organized Christianity. Even the ministers remain babes. It is impossible to be reborn spiritually and remain a babe. Once a spiritual seed is planted in fertile soil, there is no stopping the growth process. God Himself will ensure this. People delude themselves and don't even know it; they use this cop out to keep their sinister egos in place. The truth of the matter is that they aren't even babes in Christ. The truth is that they never accepted Christ. Christ said that you will know a tree by the fruit that it bears. This fruit that he spoke of are the actions that coincide with or contradict our words. Actions speak louder than words, and actions could very well say that we haven't accepted the Truth of Christ no matter what is said with the mouth. This by far is the sorriest of all cop outs: you are disgracing the Lord by using Christ's name to weasel out of your responsibilities.

Hey wait a minute!

Here are some more cop outs. Recognize any? What's the use? It makes no difference. Nothing'll ever change so why bother trying? Oh well, that's life. Maybe you have a few of your own cop outs. Recognition is crucial to their dismissal. Just recognize them as cop outs and leave it at that. No need to beat yourself up about it or try to force any action, either. Next time you find one of these or any other self created cop outs flowing through your thoughts follow it up with a, "Hey wait a minute! That's a cop out! I don't want to be a quitter!" Whenever you detect a cop out, practice following up with those last three exclamations. You can do it out loud or silently. It doesn't matter, just as long as you tell yourself in a way that makes it sound like you mean it, and leave it at that. Like I said earlier, your mind will start to get the intent and eventually give you the answers that you truly need or prompt you to take proper action.

Beliefs:

As you very well know, belief can be totally false. "I am a sucker," can be a belief, and since you believe it, your life is full of hard times and disappointments. You constantly feel sorry for yourself and are dependent on others in a way that is a hindrance to all parties involved. The enablers are just as much to blame as the dependents. If you have an erroneous belief, your life reflects the consequences of it. Hope, faulty beliefs, and mentally induced confidence (false confidence) are all products of the fake id. Faith or knowing is a product of the spirit and part of God's grace. If you were truly dwelling with the spirit, then you could never have any faulty beliefs, desperate hopes, or false confidences.

We all know that some beliefs are completely useless, but we only know this intellectually, and that is why it seems so hard to get rid of them. Intellectual knowing is useless without awareness. We have identified with these false beliefs and don't even know it. We think that we are the same as the beliefs, and now we are afraid to get rid of them. Getting rid of them would mean getting rid of ourselves. Banishing an erroneous belief system would mean banishing the false self. The false self is in charge of our mental processes (our lives). We think we are the false self; we don't realize that it is an imaginary self; when we start the process of banishing it and it thinks it is going to die, then we think we are going to die, so we fail to follow through because we don't want to destroy ourselves. We are afraid to find out who we would be without this false self. We are afraid that our lives would be without motivations, desires, fun, and most of all identities; but rest assured, to be without a false identity is the only way out. It is the only way to find yourself.

The problem with prayer and the law of attraction:

The problem with prayer and the law of attraction is this. Recall that your fake id has replaced and is masquerading as your spirit; this fake id is the imaginary ego that is equipped with an imaginary self (erroneous beliefs about yourself) and is intertwined with countless labels that you've acquired over the years about yourself and your life. These are labels that you've placed a false belief in, and they have come to life (imaginary life) and set themselves up as an entity that is enthroned in your mind. By the way, also attached to these labels are philosophies about life that you've acquired that could be totally false: life is a drag, men are insensitive dogs; women are emotional and scatter brained. Remember, it is the fake entity that is doing the praying or trying to invoke the law of attraction. You are mentally praying. You are not praying from the spirit, and your mind is filled with negative and fearful nonsense. The law of attraction in a nutshell says that like thoughts and beliefs attract the same type of circumstances. Because of your negative mental foundation, the very good that you seek is repelled no matter how much you try to imaging a favorable outcome. Yes, you can have a thought about gaining riches, but the thought has no power because of a basic negative belief system. Beliefs are the core reason for your life's circumstances. If you have a predominantly negative belief system then it will serve to counteract any positive thinking or imaging that you try to embark upon. Don't get discouraged because this condition can be remedied.

Prayer is not necessary:

Wait a minute, how can prayer not be necessary? This declaration "that prayer is not necessary" is based upon the premise that you have dissolved your fake id, and you are consciously living in spirit (the here and now). Right now, when you pray, you are probably praying with the fake id and not in spirit. In truth your spirit is whole, perfect, completely merged with God the Father and would therefore not have much to pray about. It says in the Bible that when you pray, do not use vain repetition. Most people don't know anything else but vain repetition. When I first read this scripture, "do not use vain repetition," like most folk, my imagination (fake id) kicked in. I thought that it meant to not have a memorized speech in my head for the purpose of repeating over and over. Then I thought about being a kid and saying grace in school everyday with a prayer that went something like this, "God is great, God is good, let us thank Him for our food..." and I figured that maybe this is what the scriptures were talking about as far as vain repetition goes. Not necessarily so, kids are usually innocent and sincere, so I am sure that God heard these prayers. Vain repetition is what most were taught in the church and what they were led to believe to be faith filled prayer. It doesn't have to be a memorized speech. You've seen it. Someone goes up in front of the congregation and starts to pray. It can be pretty dramatic and theatrical. Most people are bluffed into thinking that theatrics translate to real faith. Although they may be ad-libbing and they have the look of deep and sincere concern on their faces, they throw their arms up in the air with the palms facing outward and upward, and they sound honest and upright, there is also a sense of urgency in the sound and tone of their voices, but nevertheless, they are praying from their intellects and memory which translates to vain repetition or faithless prayer. These prayers usually amount to nothing and when it is realized that the prayer was fruitless, the scapegoat is, "well, it wasn't in God's Will." Here is God's will in a nutshell, so no more excuses for your faithless and vain prayers, "I wish that you may have life and have it more abundantly." You must pray from the spirit for your prayers to bear fruit, (you must pray consciously, not from mechanical dramatical theatrics) and that is all there is to it. You must enhance your faith and here is one way to do it: confession. Not before a congregation or priest or anyone else. You must admit it to yourself that you have little or no faith. What you must do in front of others is stop pretending that you have faith. Cut the pretense. Cease going along with the crowd and perpetuating the lie. You don't have to tell anyone that your faith is weak; just stop acting like you have strength when you know that you don't. Don't get discouraged because this admission is also an invitation for God to come in and grow your faith for you. Christ said because you say that you can see is the reason that you remain blind. Admit that you cannot see, and God will give you sight (author's paraphrase). You will have to start right where you are: on the level of vain repetition and praying from the mind. Start where you are and pray from your mind, and you can watch your prayers gradually grow in faith and strength to the point where you will eventually be praying from the spirit and God will be blessing you like you've never known before. All you have to do is pray like you know how but add <u>and</u> extra step. You must notice something. Notice the fakeness in your prayer. Notice the hopeful attitude, notice the doubt, notice the feeling of futility, notice the feeling of unworthiness, notice the anxiety and worry, in other words, notice the fear that accompanies your prayer. Notice the unbelief or doubt behind the pretense of faith! Oh, here is a side thought. Whenever you pray, stop saying that you are an unworthy sinner. Even if you believe yourself to be one, don't ever blurt it out again. Whenever you are in church, and your pastor leads the congregation in prayer, if he happens to say that you are unworthy sinners, do not repeat it; remain silent. By keeping quiet, you are accepting joint heir-ship with Christ. Use common sense and realize that you are either a joint heir or unworthy; you can't be both. Be bold enough to not follow the crowd and take a stand towards your own salvation. When you notice the negative thoughts, feelings, and emotions, that accompany your prayer, leave it at that. This is real confession. It is confession like you've never known or have been taught. You are going into the closet as Christ said where it is only you and God. Don't get discouraged or upset, but if you do, then notice that. It's all about self observation. Say to yourself something like this, "hmmm...ok, here comes that negative feeling again. I'm not sure what it's about, but there is no harm in looking at it, so for now, I will stop praying and watch this feeling until it fades." Then do just that: stop praying and watch the negative feeling or doubtful emotion until it fades. Do this every time you pray, and the end result will eventually be a faith filled prayer. However, it won't be the kind of prayer that you're used to. Once all doubt and negativity is removed, faith stands tall. And if you are a faith filled person, then you won't have to stop and say a speech to or plead with God. Your faith will cause another factor to come into play. Like Christ, you will be in constant communion with God, and like the scripture in the Bible that says, "God already knows before hand what you require, so he will go ahead and give it to you even before you ask." (author's paraphrase) This will be your reality, and if communion with God is your reality, then prayer as you now define it will not be necessary. If you are constantly in the bosom of God, then what could you possibly need or have to ask for? Your negative belief system will have been up rooted and cast out, and your new faith inspired belief system will automatically attract favorable circumstances in the same way that your current negative system is attracting random and unfavorable events. Having a solid faith based (egoless) belief system is what praying in spirit is all about.

Intention:

Intention is a powerful ally and once your mind understands your objective, it will cooperate, so don't try forcing it. Don't say to yourself, I was afraid again today of this person or that circumstance. Say to yourself, "it got scared again." "It," meaning your fake id (ego). Remember, you are not your mind, and therefore, you are not your thoughts, and since your ego is your thoughts about yourself, then you are not your ego. Your spirit can never be afraid. Fear is of the mind alone, so anything that makes you afraid, whether it is a minute fear or a full blown phobia, is a product of the mind's faulty imagination. Spend your day watching anything and everything impartially. Keep reminding yourself that there is a point of awareness within you that is detached from the world that can stand aside and watch the inner workings of the mind and the outer world; and you can summon it. Take a pen and pad with you and write down what produced fear in you and how you reacted. If this isn't practical, then try and remember as many of the fear producing situations that you can, and when you get home, jot them down. Once you get home, you may even realize that, you totally forgot to do the exercise and instead of observing yourself, you got absorbed into your negative imagination again. If this happens, just say "hmmm... today, I got absorbed into it again and forgot to do my observation exercise." If you say this to yourself without getting upset, then that is a good first step, if you do get frustrated, then notice your frustration (by the way, in the beginning frustration will happen a lot, so don't get discouraged; it is a normal part of the initial process) and if you do remember to observe your self, and have written down what you saw, then read over your list; once you are finished, sit in a chair or lie on your back. Try to stay as still as possible. Next, using your imagination, try to repeat as many of the fears as you can in your mind in the chronological order that they happened or as best as you can. If you flip flop the chronological order, it's not a big deal. Try to employ as best as you can all five senses: sight, sound, touch, smell, and taste. Make it as vivid as possible. Some people aren't able to visualize very well, but that's ok. If you can hear what went on or feel, this is just as good. Do this for about 5 to 10 minutes a day in an effort to make it at some point become a 30 minute daily habit. What will happen? You will start a process that will begin to dissolve the negative conditioned mind and cause your present time awareness to gradually resurface.

Book III. Reflections:

1. You are separated from God and all of Life because of internalized labels.
2. There is a difference between believing and knowing: the ego believes, the egoless knows.
3. Put first thing first. Seek the Kingdom.
4. Be patient with spiritual growth. Take the next step without any concern for the one after.
5. Diligently practice self observation.
6. You need do nothing about confusion except consciously look at it.
7. Look for God's grace in your day to day affairs and it will expand into greater miracles.
8. Miracles are possible with expanded awareness.
9. Become aware of how you resent doing the right thing and the resentment will go away.
10. Refuse to excuse yourself with copouts.
11. Use the "Hey! Wait a minute!" to combat copouts.
12. See that an intellectual knowing (memory based knowing) is not the same as awareness.
13. The issue with prayer and the "law of attraction" is the negative belief system.
14. Stop pretending to be strong when you know your faith is weak. This is the very invitation for God to come into and change your life.
15. Notice the fear and doubt that accompany your weak prayers and they will grow strong.

Book IV:

Observations and Truth:

1. Observation:
I am afraid of being afraid. Today I had to deal with a situation that normally fills me with dread and trepidation. In reality, it wasn't a harmful or dangerous situation, but then again, the source of most phobias are usually completely harmless. Yet and still, it has a powerful hold on my mind which I can't seem to shake. Upon further reflection, I realized that I was afraid of something that hasn't even occurred yet. The event that I was so afraid of was scheduled for a future date. I realized that I was afraid in the present moment of being afraid in the future. I was scared of the possibility of being scared.

Truth:
The illusion of the ego has no power at all. You only think it does, and therefore it does. Every time fear arises, remind yourself that it is an ego illusion and its menacing presence is only the pseudo power of an uncontrolled imagination.

2. Observation:
My mind is an unorganized jumbled up mess of random thoughts and imaginings. The vast majority of this mental spinning and turmoil is negativity and fantasy. Concentration and focus does not come easy for me. I don't know what to do.

Truth:
There is nothing that you can do or need to do.
Realize this fact and God will do what needs to be
done. Just impartially observe your mind's non stop
random activity and allow God to do the rest.

3. Observation:
People are quick to announce how happy they are
and how satisfied they are with their present
conditions and how truly blessed they feel;
however, the people that I know personally, when
they aren't using their tongue to voice how
wonderful things are, they are usually fussing,
quarreling, or complaining to no end about how
unfair and unjust life is. They incessantly talk about
how bad other people are. They are indeed most
miserable until I ask them how is life. And again like
magic they respond, "life is great! I am blessed."

Truth:
People are swift to tell lies about everything,
especially with regard to their personal lives. The
truth is that they lie because that is all they know.
Lying is all that they've been taught. They don't
realize that pretense and lies are the same thing.
Recognition of self lying opens the door for God's
instructions to come in.

4. Observation:
Habits are repetitious patterns of behavior that are
usually second nature to an individual: even to the
point that he can be unaware that he is performing
the action: like nail biting or leg shaking. These are
called mechanical actions. Today I caught myself

being overcome by two bad habits. One was laziness and the other procrastination. I realize that they are synonymous. Aside from fear, these are my two worse enemies. Long story short, I am my own worse enemy. It is a daily struggle to battle with these two habits: a war so to speak. It is a war that I usually end up losing.

Truth:
Stop fighting. God has already won the battle. The problem is that you give too much reverence to outward appearances and therefore become overwhelmed internally. Habits like laziness, procrastination or anything else are all ego generated. Just go about your business as best you can while constantly telling yourself this truth, stop struggling with these habits and observe them. Do this without self condemnation and God Himself will intervene, make the rough places smooth, and set you free once and for all.

5. Observation:
People are selfish and self centered. They are filled with righteous speech about helping others, supporting charity, or doing the right thing in general. But there is usually the prevalent ego thought of "what's in it for me?" People indignantly will fight for their self righteousness to the bitter end claiming that they have pure and unselfish motives. Even the author of this book use to think, "I would love for this manuscript to be a source of help to others." While his ego was thinking, "How much money will I be able to make via the sales of the publication?"

Truth:
It cannot be otherwise. As long as the ego exists, you cannot have entirely pure motives. It's the Jekyll and Hyde syndrome. God says, "Don't give too much thought to it. Just keep up with the impartial self observation and observation of others." Motives will gradually become more pure while selfishness fades away.

6. Observation:
I have accepted false doctrine. The way my life unfolds on a daily basis proves it. Sometimes in outer worldly circumstances, but the proof comes mostly from my inner mental processes. I am always battling something or someone mentally and I can't seem to shut down this process. Surely, the way to reverse it is to instill truth in my mind, but how am I to accomplish this? I need a miracle!

Truth:
You've already received your miracle. You've done your part. Honest recognition has jumpstarted your miracle. All that needs to be done now is to sit back and allow God to do His part.

7. Observation:
People secretly get warped pleasure out of other people's misery and misfortunes.

Truth:
Yes, it is a sad state of affairs. The solution is to understand that this kind of twisted pleasure serves to perpetuate your own misery. Believe it or not, you do this because you enjoy comparing

yourself with the other. You think that it gives you a sense of being ok because the other fellow is in such bad shape. The truth is that you are really no better off; you have an evil ego that is doing the comparing and enjoying the misery. The ego has tricked you into believing that you are better off. Don't buy into it. Enjoying other misery is the same as enjoying your own. Misery loves company. Once you truly see it, then you will no longer enjoy other misery because you no longer cherish your own.

8. Observation:
I am a persistent victim of pretense and idol worship. I swoon before pretty girls. I laugh at the boss' wit, even though I think it's dumb. When my closest friends and loved ones talk to me about their troubles, I put on an act of compassion and all the while, I could care less. Most of the time, I avoid them because I don't want to hear it. I am totally pretentious on the job and in public with my colleagues, friends, family, and even strangers.

Truth:
It isn't the Real You perpetrating these pretentious acts of deceit. It is the ego. Because the ego itself is fake, then everything it does can only be fake. Realize once and for all that you are not your ego, and you'll become a real person with a genuine and caring personality.

9. Observation:
I feel inadequate and inferior whenever I encounter another man that I perceive to be stronger than I, have more money and material

possessions than I, or even younger than I. I see a guy who has all sorts of benefits like popularity, good looks, and the constant company of beautiful women; I feel like I've been cheated by life.

Truth:
This happens because your ego/false self compares itself to others. Comparing can only spark feelings of inferiority and other negative states (including superiority). Even when you encounter someone with whom you believe less fortunate, you think to yourself, "how blessed am I that I am not in that predicament." The truth of the matter is that even this so called feeling of blessedness is false because it is really your ego trying to feed itself with phony images of superiority and happiness based upon its comparisons. Cease to compare and you are home free.

Book IV Reflections:

Tell yourself the truth everyday no matter what the situation is.

Book V: **Spiritology Proverbs**:

The average and the honest:

On knowing the Lord:

There is a voice that continues to whisper to everyone instructions of self correction. The honest have heeded this voice and entered the Kingdom of Heaven; the average have ignored it and descended into hell. This still small voice (your conscience) is the voice of God; hearken unto it, and you will truly get to know the Lord.

The average boasts of his relationship with God while the honest silently enjoys God's Presence.

To know the Lord is to obey the Lord, just ask the honest. The average continues to disobey, stumble, and call themselves blessed.

One cannot know the Lord and also know frustration; the honest is well acquainted with this fact. Tell the average and he will lose his religion to dispute this fact.

The honest is aware that to know the Lord coincides with getting along with people at all times and in all places. The average can know the Lord for a two hour church service and go back to bickering after the service is over.

The honest know that they know the Lord. The average believe that they know the Lord.

Knowing the Lord is the nature of the honest, for God has united with them in Spirit.

Knowing the Lord is a desperate struggle to the average for the devil dwells within their minds.

The honest are humbly ready and willing to demonstrate that they truly know the Lord; when asked for proof the average get indignant and come up with hundreds of excuses to hide their lack of faith.

God prompts the honest to go forth with their lives as a continuous testimony that they know the Lord. The devil urges the average to lie about knowing the Lord and continue to experience trials and tribulations.

For the honest, knowing the Lord is to speak in high volume with their lifestyles; for the average; knowing the Lord means using their vocal cords to loudly preach their empty and faithless sermons.

The honest are aware that the averages do not know the Lord; the average are unaware that the honest know the Lord.

The honest are calmly ready and able to be still and know the Lord; the average is nervous, afraid, and unwilling to denounce the devil.

The honest are those self aware people that have entered the Kingdom of Heaven; the average are the unaware that live in hell and don't even know it.

The average believes, "the meek shall inherit the earth." The honest know that whether meek or not, they themselves are the joint heirs with Christ; indeed, the honest truly know that even mild mannered (meek) people can be liars, thieves, hypocrites, and backstabbers.

Honest people are usually considered trouble makers; the average are labeled as model citizens.

The honest long to be Godly people without calling themselves as such; the average aspire to be Kings, Presidents, Doctors, Lawyers, etc... and use the titles to draw attention to themselves.

The average person considers an honest person judgmental or self-righteous but fails to see his own hypocrisy.

The average is quick to judge while the honest is swift to understand.

An honest person rarely follows the crowd, join clubs or clicks; even religious sects have no appeal; therefore, he is considered an outcast.

An average person desperately seeks worldly venues and organizations for his sense of identity and is deemed loyal to the common cause.

An honest person silently does not consider what others think of him, while the average individual broadcasts that he doesn't care and secretly burns with rage or self-pity if he perceives himself as being disapproved by others.

The average individual pretends that human nature isn't a factor when following rules or obeying the law; the honest person considers human nature in every area of his life's undertakings and therefore is never surprised when people in high-places do outlandish things.

An honest person never utters the phrase, "He should've known better than that or you would expect someone in that position to know better."

The average person will persecute severely anyone that breaks the rules but will excuse and make excuses for those closest to him. The honest person neither condemns nor excuses anyone for bad behavior.

A truly honest person is the happiest and most stress-free individual on the planet. His happiness is self-generated and comes from within. The average person relies on people, places, things, and events to supply his happiness. This is what accounts for the average's depression, anxiety, nervousness, and most other human ailments of a mental nature.

The average's happiness depends on fickle people, fleeting moments, and corruptible material possessions. The honest generates joy from his very nature.

The honest man seeks to understand what has happened to him while the average man seeks to vindicate.

The honest man considers all facts before deciding and acting; the average man is impulsive.

The average receives faulty advice from the ego all day long and calls it the voice of God; they constantly look for outward signs of guidance and confirmation; the honest being one with God instinctively heeds His genuine instructions through direct insight.

Only an honest person truly knows and understands that beauty (including inner beauty) is in the eye of the beholder. The average have opinions based on outward appearances.

The average person erroneously translates an honest person's patience into cowardice while the honest can clearly see the fear in back of the average's impatience.

The average man fawns before beautiful women; the honest man simply enjoys the company of a beautiful woman with no strings attached or hidden motives.

The honest are often alone but never lonely. The average constantly surround themselves with friends and loved ones while being completely absorbed in depression or loneliness.

The average openly shuns the honest but secretly seeks his wisdom and friendship. The honest are spiritually indifferent to the coming and going of the average.

The average believes that maturity comes with age; the honest know that wisdom is a gift from God that doesn't discriminate by number of years.

The average believes that he can sin all day, ask for forgiveness at night, and start the whole process again the next morning without consequences; only the honest know that consistency of right behavior that stems from a clear mind keeps him out of danger.

The average hastily complains; the honest patiently observes.

The average paints his circumstances with the color of his current emotional state; the honest impartially sees pure reality in all of its glorious splendor.

The honest fear nothing; the average is afraid of everything.

The average chases life; the honest flows with life.

The average thinks he is living his own life; the honest knows that life lives through him.

The honest are reborn everyday upon awakening to a life of beauty; the average spends his entire life worrying about death, even his sleep is infested with horrible nightmares.

The honest enjoy solitude; the average is afraid to turn off the lights at night.

The honest seeks nothing from the average; the average constantly hounds the honest.

The average craves to be loved; the honest desires to express love.

The honest adores truth; the average embrace lies.

The honest are poised, strong, and calm; the average are weak, babbling, and nervous.

The average claim God as their own Father but struggle with practicing honesty; God claims the honest as His Own children and gives them His very Own Heart and Mind.

The honest knows that all sin is equal in the eyes of God; the average believes that evil deeds can be ranked: for example lying is not as bad as stealing or murder.

The mental state of the honest is like a clear blue sky; the state of mind of the average is the same as a dark stormy night.

The average reads about, hears, and preaches Godly philosophies; the honest gets his philosophy straight from the source and therefore walks according to God's personal instructions.

The honest can adore a beautiful woman and leave it at that; the average can only lust and fears that he may not take her to bed.

The average call themselves honest; since honesty is their nature, the honest doesn't even think about the virtue of honesty.

On Heaven and Hell:

The honest have swallowed their foolish pride to enter the Kingdom of Heaven; the average would rather get in the last word during an argument and stay in hell.

Heaven is better than anyone could ever hope for or imagine; hell is worse than even your greatest fears and nightmares could be.

To go to Heaven you (your ego self) must be crucified: Crucifixion of the ego results in resurrection of the Real Self; in this way the honest have ascended to Heaven; preservation of the ego has disastrous consequences which sends the average into the abyss.

The average thinks that you die (experience physical death) and then go to Heaven; the honest know that the Kingdom of Heaven is in the here and now even while dwelling on the earthly plane, and that the ego must die to ascend to Heaven on Earth and into the beyond.

The average fears the possibility of going to hell when he dies and all the while lives his earthly existence in a self-created hell. Hell doesn't even exist to the honest since he already dwells in the Kingdom of Heaven.

Since the honest already dwell in Heaven, he has nothing to achieve while on Earth; the average desperately tries to achieve on Earth before he dies and goes to Heaven.

Heaven and hell are opposite sides of the same coin.

Heaven is spiritual awareness; hell is mental absorption.

Heaven is severely under populated; hell is standing room only.

Entering hell is easy, takes no effort, and yields no dividends; just observe the lazy average; entering the Kingdom takes some effort but once in, everything is provided for you; the honest can vouch for this.

You can't go to Heaven; Heaven comes to (is already within) you; likewise, you can't go to hell; it comes to (is generated from within) you.

Heaven is unlimited; it is within, without, and all around you; hell is finite and expands only as far as your imagination.

All who enter Heaven enjoy bountifully its perpetual incessant bliss; those that go to hell suffer from a countless multitude and variety of terrors.

All who want to enter Heaven can easily ask to do so, but your request must be sincere; you may as well ask because whether you ask for it or not, the alternative is hell. Go ahead. Ask.

There is no happy medium or neutral zone; at this very moment, you dwell in either Heaven or hell. If you are uncertain about this or deny it, then you most certainly are in hell.

If you really want to escape from hell, for starters, you can stop all the pretentious nonsense with your fellow citizens of hell that all is well; if you want to enter the Kingdom of Heaven then you must first see that you are in hell.

The only reason why a man remains in hell is because he thinks it is Heaven.

Heaven is eternal; hell is temporary.

On God and the Devil:

The honest are the true servants of God; the average are slaves to the devil.

The honest have found favor and gained friendship with God; the average has sold his soul to the devil without even reading the fine print on the contract that says, "Your soul is worthless to me; therefore, thou shall have nothing in return."

God consistently prompts the honest to demonstrate their faith in the here and now; the devil urges the average to brag about and embellish past exploits.

The devil exploits the average; God takes care of the honest.

God knows all of the devil's motivations; the devil desperately tries to decipher the will of God: contrary to popular beliefs, the devil knows nothing about God's will.

The devil's goal is to destroy the average and use the average to tempt the honest; God's plan is for the honest to be living examples to the average.

The average is urged by the devil to indignantly fight for what is right; the honest refuses to fight because he knows that God has already won the battle.

The honest is aware that he dwells in the bosom of God; the average is unaware that the devil dwells within his own neurotic mind.

To calmly know oneself is to know God; those that are quick to anger are well acquainted with the devil.

The devil possesses the average; God indwells the honest.

God blesses the honest; the devil punishes the average.

The devil demands more and more from the average while constantly bestowing upon him greater and greater punishment; God only requires that the honest sit back and faithfully receive incessant blessings.

The honest trusts and allows God to handle his daily affairs; the average spends his days cowering to and serving the devil.

God has opened the eyes of the honest; the average have been hypnotized and put to (spiritual) sleep by the devil.

The average believes in the devil's pseudo power and remains weak; God renews the strength of the honest daily and lifts him up.

The honest abide by the Grace of God; the average are trapped within the devil's delusions.

God comforts the honest; the devil torments the average.

God commands the devil and His will is done; the devil demands from God but gets cast from His Presence.

God never thinks about the devil; the devil is fearfully obsessed with God.

The average will never admit that they don't know God thereby remaining with the devil whose only gift to them is foolish pride; the honest were once average who grew weary of the devil's devices and humbled themselves before God Whose gift to them is Heaven.

The devil is always attempting to find ways of impersonating God in an effort to fool the masses of average and further advance the vast empire of hell; God is always Himself; and with everlasting patience, He continues to build His Kingdom one soul at a time.

The devil hates both the honest and average; he knows that he can't escape hell and enter Heaven which is why he desperately tries to destroy souls; God loves the average just as much as he does the honest but can't save them unless they really want salvation.

The devil causes the average to believe that God's salvation is achieved simply by faithlessly saying you have it; the honest know that deliverance comes by internal faithful unwavering acceptance alone.

The devil uses the average to slander the honest; God uses the honest to consol the average.

The devil is temporal and cannot exist without the average's belief in him; God is eternal and existed before the creation of man.

God is the final reality of everything that exists; the devil is a product of imagination and fades in and out of existence depending on the thoughts of men.

Real Christians and Church Folks:

Real Christians are silently victorious; church folks are loud boastful victims.

Real Christians rarely join up with any organized religion; church folks are lifetime members of their chosen religious sects.

Real Christians are reborn once and as Christ said on the cross, "it is finished." Church folks constantly succumb to feelings of guilt and rededicate themselves to Christ over and over and over again.

Real Christians never put other human beings on pedestals; church folks often boast about their pastors being good men or men of God.

Real Christians refuse to exult other human beings; church folks celebrate pastor anniversaries and other such blasphemous nonsense in the church.

Real Christians know the Bible for its message and live their lives accordingly; church folks are prideful of memorizing Bible verses and quoting them to impress each other.

Real Christians speak truth no matter what the consequences; church folk make excuses and tell lies just to save their own hides.

Church folks are quick to say, "I know the Lord or I've found Jesus." Real Christians know that Christ Himself wouldn't even bother to enter most churches of today.

Real Christians know from experience that "The Kingdom of Heaven is at hand." Church folks are not aware that Christ was referring to them when he said, "I never knew you."

Church folks call themselves "real Christians." Real Christians do not label themselves at all. They don't even call themselves "Christian."

 A Real Christian minister is like a breath of fresh air to his congregation and always take into consideration every aspect of their welfare; therefore, he will never pressure them in anyway whatsoever: especially financially for God has already provided for his needs including the upkeep of his church;

Church folk pastors are spiritual and financial vampires that constantly guilt trip their congregations to empty their wallets so that they can fatten their own. A church folk pastor will throw every scripture in the Bible at you in order to continuously drain your bank account. They purposely refuse to consider the Bible verses of 2nd Corinthians, Chapter 8, verses 12 and 13. Read it, and ask yourself if you've ever heard any minister quote it. You may find some relief for yourself.

A church that is constantly passing around a collection plate to collect money to make ends meet is a faithless church with a faithless pastor.

 Real Christians know that the sum total of your thoughts and behavior is what your religion really is; Church folk think that fellowship within a religious sect is one of the requirements for getting into Heaven.

Real Christians know God by way of direct communion; church folk have the illusion of knowing God through their imagination.

Real Christians are spiritual and place mental activity in its proper secondary place; church folk confuse mental activity with the spiritual.

Real Christians know that true charity does not mean to get taken advantage of; church folk are easily fooled and spiritually drained by moochers in the name of their very own religion.

Real Christians know that the only cross to bear until it is crucified is the ego; church folk foolishly and arrogantly believe that it literally means to bear the troubles of the world upon themselves. How silly it is to think that you have the spiritual muscle to do what Christ did.

Church folk think that their purpose in life is the same as Christ's; Real Christians know that Christ is the Way Shower and has done all the hard grunt work for them.

Real Christians know that Salvation is truly a free gift that they can have through faith and acceptance; church folk stubbornly harbor their subconscious notions that they must earn salvation with worldly deeds: going to church, giving to charity, tithing, etc. They foolishly believe that it all counts for something, and that their neurotic negative mindsets can be overlooked.

Real Christians know that all men are of God and treat them the same; church folk believe their pastors, preachers, ministers, priests, deacons, etc... are men of God and give them special privileges.

The Bible:

The average takes both old and new testament principles and weaves his life into a complicated web of confusion and despair. The honest considers Christ and only Christ and turns his life into a haven of bliss.

The Bible Says,
"Faith without works is dead." Only the honest truly knows the inner, deeper, and much richer meaning of this. This is why an honest person knows that works without real sincerity and faith have no merit in the Eyes of God.

To the honest, the Bible is a book of profound truths; to the average it is a book of fairy tales.

For the honest, the Bible is a master piece of spiritual deliverance; to the unaware average, it is a cruel doctrine of unendurable bondage.

The honest consider it a joy to read and study the Bible; to the average it is a hard painstaking chore that will never get done.

The honest read the Bible to promote their own spiritual growth; the average read the Bible to preach it to others.

The words of the Bible are filtered through the thick and dull egos of the average causing them to live lives of strife and chaos; the same Biblical instructions mesh with the inner knowing of the egoless honest whom lead harmonious lifestyles pleasing and approved by the Lord.

The average read the Bible and joins organized

religions. The honest read also but refuse to get involved with these dangerous cults.

The honest uses the Bible to point the way to salvation. The average exploit the scriptures for the selfish purpose of justifying his own sin and hypocrisy.

To really understand the Bible, the ego must be shed. The honest realizes this fact and has made it his ultimate goal; the average dimly suspects it but has no intention of taking the risk.

The honest receives insight from God and understands both the literal and metaphorical aspects of the Bible. The average interprets through his egotistical memory and imagination and also accept the demented opinions of their average ministers, so therefore have no choice but to consider it all literal.

The average read the Bible and claim satan as their adversary; the honest read the Bible and dismisses all attachments to the devil.

The average will read a few scriptures and therefore consider himself an expert in telling you how to best relate to God. The honest will study the bible and advise to let God relate to you.

The average read the Bible and become self righteous; the honest read the Bible and humbly follow God.

The average read the Bible and are always called to preach. The honest read the Bible and are called to preach, teach, heal, and minister.

It is possible for the average to have the Bible fully memorized but not understood. It is possible for the honest to have the Bible fully understood but not memorized.

To the average, memorization of the scripture is top priority; to the honest, understanding the meaning of scripture is most important.

The average may carry Bibles around wherever they go; the honest may not even own a Bible.

The average believe that the Bible is the one and only source for true spirituality; the honest know that the Source Himself is within hearts and not from a book.

The average will use the Bible along with long wordy desperate prayers to rebuke satan; the honest can scare off the devil with a quick glance.

The average read the Bible and think they can summon Angels to their earthly aid while the honest know that God Himself is their keeper.

The average believe that regular reading of the Bible is loyalty to God; the honest simply walks with God and may go without even seeing a Bible for months at a time.

The average think that memorizing the Bible constitutes a strong rock solid relationship with God; the honest know that communion is the only way.

The average think they will go to Heaven by reading and memorizing the Bible. The honest have already entered the Kingdom by following the instruction of the Bible.

On Angels and Demons:

An angel is the ministering spirit of God; a demon is a conniving minion of the devil.

Here are some names of Angels:
Self-Awareness is the archangel and some of his top loyal officers are as follows:
Honesty, Integrity, Courage, Happiness, Enthusiasm, Loyalty, Vigor.

Here are some names of demons:
Fear is the king of demons, and some of his demonic henchmen are as follows: anger, depression, loneliness, frustration, boredom, confusion, jealousy, bitterness, guilt.

Angels are assigned to the honest; demons latch on to the average.

To see an Angel, all an honest man has to do is look in the mirror; to see a demon, likewise, the average man can do so by looking in the mirror.

Angels come to the aid of and comforts the honest without fail; by the same token, demons trip up the average and then laughs and taunts him after he falls on his face.

Angels are gentle and strong; demons are weak and vicious.

Angels are on guard 24/7 making sure that the honest are safe and secure; demons work around the clock leading thieves, liars, and even killers to the doorstep of the average.

Angels keep demons away from the honest thereby maintaining their spiritual freedom;
demons disguise themselves as angels to keep the average in their hellish bondage.

Angels uplift the honest while demons trample the average.

Angels have no ulterior motives and are joyfully content to pamper the honest; demons cruelly plot and scheme against the average to satisfy their own twisted pleasures.

An Angel will never make a promise to the honest; no need, since it and the honest are woven from the same cloth, trust is the nature of the relationship; a demon forever makes false vows to the average, and all the while it anxiously awaits and anticipates the disappointment of its gullible victim.

Demons wage war against Angels; contrary to
popular belief, Angels don't do battle with demons.

Angels will protect the honest from demons;
demons don't go near the honest because even the
thought of an Angel's presence terrifies it.

It is because of demonic influence that the average
face the threat of danger at every turned corner.

Demons haunt the average even in their
dreams; Angels preserve the honest in reality.

Any man that refutes praise and does his work well
for the sheer joy of it is an Angel; a man that
accepts praise is an ego driven demon that enjoys
the spotlight; if he does his work well, it is because
he craves attention and pats on the back.

On Idol Worship & Worship:

The average confuses idol worship with Godly love;
the honest knows that love of God is to truly
worship God.

The average crave to be worshipped. The honest
delight in worshipping God.

The average cower before their bosses: doing
favors for them out of pseudo respect, fear, or
hope of better days and higher positions; the
honest are not materialistic because they don't

need to be; they know that to have God is the whole point of life.

The average form false camaraderies in order to feel superior and accepted; the honest are usually considered islands but are united with the whole Universe.

The average feign before their spouses in an effort to please; the honest have no pretense or need for idol worship so their only agenda is enjoying the Presence of God.

The average get married in order to form bonds and unions to become united as one; whenever the honest are wedded, that union extends beyond the two individuals and throughout the whole Universe.

The average worship God by getting on bended knee saying speeches of praise, deliverance, and petitions. The honest worship God by treating people right and being what they are (honest).

The average see God as a being in the sky looking down upon them for attention; the honest experience God from within, without, around, above, below and basks in His Holy Presence.

The average have a daily monotonous routine of begging and pleading for redemption; the honest have submitted and therefore received salvation.

The average can fathom no other way of worship and have therefore turned God into a sadistic tyrant; the honest practice true worship by positioning themselves to receive their due blessings.

The average are too stubborn and scared to let go of their primitive worshipping ways; the honest have courageously let go of everything they had in order to have it all.

The average get kicked around in life, blame the devil for it, and pray to God for vengeance while clinging to their devilish ways and mindsets; the honest know no such hardships nor are they acquainted with the devil; paradise is all they know and have.

The average worship God as subordinates; the honest commune with God as a co-creators.

Book VI:

Exercises for Spiritual Growth:

Here is an exercise with prayer and the law of attraction that if done with self honesty, (without getting upset at what you see: can't stress this point often enough) will eventually cause your prayers and mental wishes to become more powerful and magnetic.
Notice that no matter how powerfully you focus your thoughts or how much fervor you pray with that there is an underlying doubt or wondering or hoping that it will work or come to pass. Again, without judgment, notice how you tend to imagine the way God will bring about the answer or how you envision it coming about or happening. You do not need to assist God in His handy work, and this exercise will help you to get rid of this prayer dousing habit. This impartial self observation technique will work wonders for your prayer life. Pray often as you can. Mental prayer is like rolling the dice or winning the lotto. Your prayers coming to pass is all about chance or luck, but if you pray continuously while observing your doubt, then the doubt will start to dissolve and your prayers will become more and more fruitful. They will become more and more answered because you will be praying more and more in spirit as opposed to praying with a negative mind. This exercise will be a great enhancement to your prayer life. You may be pleasantly surprised to find out that this exercise will even help to eliminate desperate and compulsive desires. You will be amazed to come to

conclusions like: why did I want that in the first place? I never needed it. What a relief. Now you're growing up spiritually!

Another exercise:

As you go through your day, notice how you or other people label themselves. For instance, someone may introduce himself as a doctor or manager. Try to see that they actually believe in these labels as opposed to using them for outward identification. Notice how they are feeding their insatiable egos by internalizing their labels. This is a mental health producing exercise, so practice as often as possible. You can even observe how you yourself have labels that you believe are the real you. Another thing to notice is the emotional reaction if someone contradicts or confirms your labels or someone else's labels. For instance, you or someone else is a manager or something of the sort. Notice how it makes you feel good or upset, depending on what the other person's opinion is. The person may say I think you are a good mother or a bad father. It either brings up good feelings, which is false vanity, or ill feelings. Either way, it proves that an individual believes in and thereby is at the mercy of the labels and separated (mentally only) from God. You think to yourself, "I am a doctor; therefore, there is me, the doctor, and God." Remember, Christ was always announcing, "I and the father are One," You should do the same.

Affirmations:

You really can't talk yourself into a greater spiritual reality, but you can watch yourself evolve into one. You can do this through affirmations based on truth as opposed to worldly decrees. If you don't know what a truth based affirmation is, then read the four gospels. They are peppered with them. For instance, you can say, "God is my Loving Father; I and my Father are One." You can say what Christ said without hesitation for remember you are "joint heirs." You can also say, "If God is for me, then who or what can be against me?" These affirmations are based in truth as opposed to, "I am wealthy or I am confident," which are worldly affirmations; face it, if you are poor or living from paycheck to paycheck, and you worry about your day to day affairs, then you will not be very successful with these worldly (ego based) statements. These worldly statements may be in conflict with your present time reality. You may even feel that you are lying to yourself and grow more frustrated with your present circumstances; if you say truth based affirmations, then you can't conjure up any mental contradictions, but you may notice something similar: a sort of mental discomfort or anxiety. Most people will mistake it as worry or doubt but don't be fooled. This is a good sign. What's happening is that you are starting the process of causing your old and faulty belief system (ego) to collapse by shaking it at its foundation. It is the ego's anxiety of being toppled by truth. If you experience this discomfort, (that is sometimes even disguised as doubt) then here is

112

what you can do. As you say your truth based affirmations, notice the discomfort as it starts to arise. Just watch it. Once the discomfort arises, stop the affirmations and just be with the discomfort. Just let it be there and watch it until it fades. Once it fades, start back with your affirmations. If the discomfort arises again, then repeat the process. In time, the discomfort will continue to arise but it will get less and less intense until it is totally dissolved and comes up no more. Once this happens, powerful and practical truths will be implanted in your psyche that will produce amazing things for you in your life.

Fear ridding techniques:
Fear broken down:

Fear is a by product of the false self. It is the false self: plain and simple. Take away all the psychological mumbo jumbo and see fear for what it really is. It is a feeling; correct? Yes, it is. I'm sure you'll at least agree with that. It is a most unpleasant feeling. No one needs a degree in psychology to know this. Fear and confidence are the same thing. Confidence is just another label conjured up by the false self in an effort to keep itself going by disguising fear. To take it from the top, the false self is a mass of beliefs about your life combined with countless labels of yourself and emotionalizations about these labels. The nature of the false self is a sense of separation. I am "so and so." You are someone else. I am me and you are you. We are two different individuals and therefore must compete with each other in someway. It is

113

you against me. To believe in separation means to compare and with the comparisons, something has to win out. Something has to be better or worse than something else. Here is where fear comes in. For the most part, the false self is comparing everything and everyone to itself. It compares itself to other people and comes to the conclusion that it is either superior or inferior to the other. It is looking for security through comparing. It compares itself to situations and circumstances and decides that it is either adequate or inadequate in facing or handling the situation or circumstance. With all the comparing constantly going on, it has no choice but to produce fear because the comparing causes the questioning of, "Can I cope or can I survive." The moment you ask a question of this nature is the very same moment that you've forgotten God. When you forget about God, the devil (fear) then rears its ugly head. The false self worries and all the while comparing that it may not be able to handle something or measure up to someone. During the comparison processes the false self can only view the compared event, circumstance, or person, as a threat. When threats are perceived, fear has no choice but to emerge. The reason why you are always scared is because the ego is always comparing itself to anything and anyone outside of itself. Whenever it gets a few victories over circumstances or other people, it stores these pseudo victories and stockpiles them in the memory and makes more comparisons; now it calls itself superior to others or circumstances based upon these memorized victories. Now it thinks that it has proof that it is superior and it calls itself confident. Sooner or later, a defeat comes about and the ego now sees that it was inferior to or inadequate to a circumstance or situation. Now it considers itself inferior. This is all wrong. By its very nature, the ego is the exact opposite of what you really are: your Real Self. The Real Self is confident without having to think or compare. The false self always looks to compare in order to justify its existence or validate itself. The Real Self simply exists. The false self is about separation while the Real Self has a sense of unification with all. How can you be afraid of anything if you are unified with it? It is impossible. The phony self has setup camp inside your mind and doesn't want to leave or be evicted. Since you think that you are this phony self, the comparing that it does causes you fight and battle with circumstances and people because you think they are threats. You create these fake enemies and perceive that you must do battle with them in order to do away with fear, but this only magnifies fear. Yes, you create stress producing and fearful fictitious situations and enemies, so that you can fight phony battles to get rid of the fear that you've generated in the first place. You go though this maddening routine of comparing in order to prove that you are real. You subconsciously think that you are handling your life's affairs (solving problems, etc...) when in reality, you are being robotically manipulated and controlled by an illusory ego. You feel responsible for handling your life as opposed to allowing God to live it for you. The comparing makes you scared, so you view everything outside of yourself as hostile. You then attempt to fight in some way in order to defend yourself. Whatever you do, depending on the outcome, whether it is to cringe before someone, run away, hide, fight or yell back, you see it as a victory or defeat: all the while not realizing that it is all defeat. You then move on to the next circumstance or person to compare yourself with and start the whole process all over again. The day you stop the comparing is the day fear goes away forever.

Fear is pain and (emotional) pain is fear:

They are synonymous or one and the same, and your mind is totally engulfed by both. You will at some point have to be willing to see this fact if you want to achieve self healing. Stop pretending that you are ok when you know that you are suffering. You go out in public and pretend to be strong, confident, and level headed. Then, when the show is over, you go home to yourself and suffer in private. Stop with the lies and nonsense. Don't you realize that you are confusing your mind and blocking your very own healing processes? This is like pulling the scalp off of a wound. Keep it up, and not only will it never heal, but it will eventually become infected and the infection will spread. Yes, by being pretentious, you are slowly driving yourself insane. This is what a false (lying) nature does. Self lying causes resentment and guilt to build within and eventually causes the individual to become neurotic. When you tell another that you are ok when you're really not, your mind accepts your word and doesn't do a thing to heal you. It accepts this contradiction as truth. It reasons, "well, he said that he's ok, so there is nothing for me to do about the condition." You put up with great internal struggles to keep this facade alive just to be impressive to others and your mind believes that this is what you want. Tell yourself the truth; tell your mind the truth so that it will come to your aid with emotional healing. It will start to view fear as an invader instead of a resident and begin the eviction process.

Just like the body, the mind is designed by God to be a self healing mechanism. Stop pretending that you are ok for the sake of appearances. Stop telling people, "I'm doing great," whenever you are feeling lousy. You don't have to say, "I'm feeling lousy today," but if you do, make sure it isn't a ploy for sympathy which will draw even more negativity from the other person, and don't forget to impartially observe the feeling of lousiness (very important to consciously notice the ill feeling). An honest, but neutral statement would be something like, "I'm making the best of it." It is honest and doesn't invite sympathy or negativity from others. It also sends a message to your mind that you are giving it permission to help you. Self honesty is very important. Because you lie about your condition, the mind doesn't believe that it needs to be healed. Because you lie, your mind thinks that you really want the pain (people subconsciously covet their pain and misery). Your mind houses a massive amount of pain and fear that are mostly attached to distant and sometimes recent memories. Your mind knows that you fear the fear and pain and anything you perceive as being painful or fearful.

You are afraid of your fears and pain; you believe that they can't be remedied; your mind masks the fear and pain so that you can better cope with it. It provides you with so-called defense mechanisms. Yes, you believe that your fear and pain can't be cured; otherwise you would've been healed perhaps years ago. If you do believe that healing is possible, then you value the pain in some way. You must quit loving your sickness. You are attached and addicted to your pain, fears, misery, and suffering.

Your mind is always trying to push pain and fear up from your subconscious depths to the surface so that pain can be expelled and fear dissolved.

Since you fear the pain and you fear the fear, your mind has designed clever ways to push up these painful and fearful emotions; thereby allowing the healing process to happen. Yes, the mind is doing its part, but you are not doing your part as far as healing goes. One way fear is perpetuated is through negative mental pictures. Another way is through labeling the fear (calling it something else); you attach labels to fear and pain such as anger, depression, loneliness, boredom, frustration, 'false' excitement, shyness, or any other negative emotion you can think of. This self labeling gives the illusion of fear being part of your God given spiritual essence (your true identity).

If you really think about these emotional labels, backtrack, and do a little investigating, you will eventually conclude that they are all forms of fear. You think they are your personality traits, so they remain and continue to torture you. These negative attributes are not your natural personality; you somehow picked them up along the way by believing in their reality. Think about an intense fear that you may have. This fear may be labeled as a phobia. You think that you are afraid of an outside circumstance like heights or public speaking, but you are not. You are afraid of the thought. Your mind uses the circumstance as a catalyst to bring the fear to the surface, but you are still afraid of the thought. If you were to take the fear-thought away about the height or public speaking, the circumstance would still be there but the phobia would not exist.

You don't recognize what your mind is trying to do, so you either wallow in the fear, get absorbed in the mental pictures of what may happen which causes a reaction called panic, or you suppress. These are unhealthy reactions, and suppression by far, is the worst thing you can do. The more you suppress a fear, the stronger your belief in the feared thing becomes and the more it imprisons and controls you. Also, the more likely you are to attract the thing feared to you.

"The thing I greatly feared has come upon me."
Book of Job 3:25.

In conclusion, you are afraid of yourself because you believe that your fear is who you are. You believe that the fear is your identity. You take the clause, "I am," and attach it to a label or a fear: I am afraid of heights. Stop saying "I am afraid of anything!" Start telling yourself the truth. It is the truth that sets you free. If the emotion or fear comes to the surface of your mind be honest and say, "I feel afraid." Don't say, "I am afraid." This is how you begin to detach from irrational fear. Remember that the mind is self healing, and if you say, "I am afraid," then the mind reasons, "well this is what I am, so there is nothing that can be done but to live with fear (myself) and cope as best as I can; this is painful and unpleasant, but I can't get rid of myself." If you say something like, "I feel afraid," then the mind reasons, "I really don't like this feeling, so I will drop it because it is painful, and I don't like pain." Thus, the healing process begins. Get rid of fear by ceasing to identify with it and you are spiritually reborn!

You may believe that you have dozens, hundreds, or even thousands of fears; however, in reality, you have only one fear. The fear of yourself (your ego is afraid of itself). The mental household of fear has many imaginary rooms, cellars, corridors, attics, and closets: fear of heights, public speaking, death, darkness, etc...but it is all an illusion (one illusion with the appearance of multiplicity). There is only one house and that house is your imagination. Here is a way to dissolve the fear of yourself. Each time you face a fear (the feeling itself) head on with conscious awareness, you diminish it. You can simply be (consciously) aware of fear and gradually watch it fade out of existence. Practice frequently. The more you do so the swifter your progress.

1. Worry Watchers:

People are naturally curious; aren't they? They are what you would call "watchers." Rightfully so, because it is a God given trait. It is by watching that we truly learn. By watching or observing, facts collect in the mind and become memory, and the memory can serve us with points of reference for guidance on how to handle day to day affairs. This could be good or bad depending on if negative emotions are attached to the memorized data. Some folks are bird watchers. Some people (like the author) are into watching marine life; there are even those who people watch. People are fascinated with watching nature. However, out of all those nature and people watchers, probably only a handful are self watchers or watchers of inner human nature. Become a self watcher and you are guaranteed to soar to the heights of spirituality. Be a fear or worry watcher. You won't be sorry. There are probably fears that you continuously face on a daily basis or repetitive worries that plague your mind pretty frequently. You are continuously tormented by these repetitious anxieties. From now on, do something different. Don't try to fight, suppress, or ward them off but watch them instead. Let your fears and worries rise to the surface of your mind so that you can simply watch them. Since they are there anyway, you may as well. You have nothing to lose except fear itself. Now, you may think that you do this already, but again you are mentally self absorbed in your anxiety. You must be aware. As best as you can, use your conscious awareness to watch these fears without being self absorbed. Sometimes it can be a challenge, especially when you are in the midst of an intense fear that is literally shaking you up. If this is the case, come to the exterior and become aware of your physical reactions: shaking knees, sweaty palms, pounding heart, stuttering speech, or any other type of nervous bodily function. Watching the outside of yourself is just as valuable. If you are new to this technique, then watching your physical reactions is probably easier. Watch your fears; watch your worries, and watch them pack their bags and move out of your mental household forever.

2.   Watch nature of others:

Sometimes, especially in the beginning, it may be hard to shake the self absorption and watch your inner mental mechanics, especially when you are in the midst of a fear and mentally are being smacked back and forth like a tennis ball. A technique that you can use that will assist you in becoming skilled at watching yourself is to watch others. A good place to start is to study their facial expressions. I am sure that you know people who are always gloomy, angry, bitter, nervous, (well, they are all nervous and scared) but watch these people that make a habit out of doom and gloom. Passively watch how they are so intensely self absorbed. This will assist you in noticing your own self absorption. Notice how some people are perpetually positive. You ask them how they are doing and they respond something like this, "I am doing great!" Afterwards, just notice how their facial expressions tell a different story. See the contradictions. Notice the tense looks of people: the looks of anxiety or worry, the hardened and angry faces. Notice how some people giggle or laugh mechanically after every statement; the so called positive and happy ones are fakers too. It is good to notice the fakers. Don't get emotionally judgmental about them or discouraged in anyway. Just watch and notice with a sense of curiosity. You will be hit with a realization that the majority of people, no matter what they say or how they try to fool you, are living in their own self created misery. You will see clearly that beyond trying to deceive you, they are really trying to fool themselves. This will help you to see how you lie to yourself, and when you clearly see the lies, the lies evaporate.

3. Daily fear facing:

Coping mechanism:

The number one coping mechanism used to deal with fear is nothing more than pretense. People are pretending to not be afraid. Not only does this keep the fear in place, but it fuels the fear thereby making it stronger over time. The more you pretend to be unafraid, (which is the same as suppressing the fear) the greater the acceptance or belief in the fear. This is why it intensifies over time. Some people hide from fear, which is quite silly, because you take yourself (the frightened mind) wherever you go to seek refuge. The fear never goes away; it only recoils into the subconscious where it continues to build its strength and imaginary power over you.

Fear is a battle: an imaginary battle. It is fought by an imaginary self on the imaginary battle ground of your mind's imagination. You imaging yourself to be fighting against the world, but in reality, it is an inner war and a self inflicted battle: your ego verses your true self. You can stop fighting anytime you want, but you do not realize that because other people around you are fighting their personal inner battles too. You falsely perceive that they are bringing the battle to you, so you remain engaged in conflict. In essence, your true self never fights, so it is your ego attempting to keep the real you from emerging. All you need do is see and understand the nature of the battle (what it is and where it is) and the war is over.

Fear is a demon that dwells in your mind. This demon has tricked you into believing that it is a part of your essential self (spiritual being). If you truly knew or were acquainted with your true (spiritual) being, then there is no way your mind could house one single fear. You have a belief or many beliefs about life. They are wrongful, detrimental, (selfish egotistical), and in some cases deadly beliefs, but you think they are truthful and necessary for survival. The belief that all the other wrongful beliefs are necessary for life is the ring leader (the king) of the wrongful beliefs. These wrongful beliefs have been appointed by the demon fear and have taken over (replaced your spiritual being) as the navigators in your life's journey. These wrongful beliefs are coconspirators with the demon fear. The coconspirators act as double agents. They take Christ's friendly message of salvation and cause you to disregard, warp, misinterpret, or distort it. In essence, they cause you to believe that you are saved when you really are not. The wrongful beliefs intercept the message, taint it, and give it back to you contaminated. Now you clash with any and everyone as a result while claiming a Christlike nature, and you remain in sin. The demon fear then tempts you to justify remaining in sin. It is indeed a satanic merry-go-round. The demon fear has many "thought" weapons at its disposal: these weapons include anxiety, panic, depression, worry, hostility, etc. The wrongful navigators size up whatever circumstances you are dealing with in the moment and instruct the demon fear with which weapon to attack you with. For instance, if you have to meet with the boss, the navigator tells the demon, "Oh oh, the boss has summoned you, load up the thought gun with the 'anxiety' shells and be prepared to fire UPON YOUSELF as soon as you walk in the door." Or maybe, your phone hasn't rang in several days, another wrongful navigator will say, "Hmmm, no one appreciates you. Break out the 'depression' bomb and blow up everything in sight, including YOURSELF. Follow up the attack with the 'anger' pistol. Call some people, give them a piece of your mind and find out why they are neglecting you." The demon fear's only goal and reason for existing is to keep you anxious, scared, miserable, and eventually destroy you. Dislodge these traitors (wrongful beliefs) from your mind; consequentially your true spiritual being will emerge and annihilate the demon fear thereby regaining control of your (its) life.

The cure for all fear:

In truth, your fears are only imaginary defenses and coping mechanisms created by your ego; these fears are designed to ensure the ego's existence and dominance over your life but in truth, they have no bases in reality and they have no power over you; but you think they do and feel they must remain hidden (this is part of what perpetuates fear) to believe that you should hide your fear equates to protecting your fear; if you protect your fear then your mind takes it as wanting to keep the

126

fear installed; you feel the fear must remain hidden because you believe that you will be perceived as the weak and phony individual (by others) that you already believe yourself to be; if you didn't really think that you were weak and inadequate, you'd have virtually no fear; but you believe in your perceived weakness, so you desperately suppress your fear. You don't have to think you're strong. Just don't buy into weakness. Ironically, it is the hiding of your fears that gives them power to terrorize you because the suppression is an indication that you believe in their reality and ability to harm you or make your life miserable. When you suppress, you cower and bow down to fear (a false god), and simultaneously increase its imaginary hold on you. Exposure is the cure. When the light of exposure (without any mental resistance) takes place, the darkness of fear is dispersed. Here is the formula for any situation that causes fear.

Let yourself be afraid, simultaneously (consciously) know that you are being afraid, and don't try to be unafraid.

Gradually fear will dissolve and you will be naturally unafraid: without fear. There will be no suppression because there won't be anything to suppress, and you will know it without question. If you remember, the Perfect God designed you to be a perfectly functioning being while here on the planet, and that means you were predesigned to be unafraid.

Fear and becoming fearless:

On a few occasions I've heard an acronym for fear that made sense at the time I first heard it, but after more personal self study, I concluded that the acronym (although it had some merit) wasn't totally accurate. Why? Because like most self help programs and systems, it seemed to be attempting to recondition, desensitize, hypnotize, change, make positive, or rehabilitate an already phony (imaginary) ego which is impossible to do. What needs to be done with the ego is to put it through a process of gradual dissolution by impartially observing it and its activity. You must see through it. This is really the only thing you can do about fear simply because fear is a product of the unbridled imagination. Attempting to do otherwise, like confronting an outside concrete source, usually serves to solidify the belief in the fear's reality. Light (awareness-consciousness) dispels darkness (fear: the unconscious ego).

Accurate information is very crucial when it comes to dealing with any issue of a psychological nature. All psychological problems are fear based. Since psychological problems are all generated and perpetuated by the ego or self image then we must logically conclude that the ego is not only the source of all fear but it is all fear. Not only that, but it is also the ego that is attempting to remedy the very fear that it generates because it is afraid (an endless chasing of the tail).

It is the fear itself that is trying to be unafraid.

128

Now you can easily see why psychological problems not only persist but for some folks they never go away. They endure them to the day they die; they may go through life pretending to not be afraid or suppressing fear (which is the same thing). They eventually develop an erroneous belief that suppression of fear is the same as being fearless. It never dawns on a so-called fearless individual that the reason he needs pep talks is because he suppresses fear. Pretending to not be afraid (suppression) is the only remedy that the ego can offer; it is a destructive remedy and is why so many people are stressed out, nervous, antsy, neurotic and even psychotic, so what is needed is healthy a dosage of truth. The truth must get past the ego and its self preservation defenses to your inner essence (spirit) to where it can be used to free your real inner being. The sinister ego has a multitude of clever and convincing evasions and defenses to ward off truth in order to keep itself in tact (secure within your psyche). Truth is truth and it cannot be changed or altered. Since an ego or self image can be altered, then logic dictates it isn't truth or real. Therefore fear cannot be real. That acronym that I first heard is as follows: Fear = False evidence appearing real. A concern that I have with this acronym is the "who" that the evidence is appearing real to. Only an ego can be afraid therefore, the thing that his doing the viewing isn't real. Another concern I have with this acronym is the second word "evidence." Since the evidence that produces the fear is a matter of perception, then it may or may not be false. It is generally understood that it is a thought about the evidence that produces fear, and not the actual evidence itself. So if a man is afraid of heights, he may be on a hiking trip with some friends and come upon a mountain. His fear of heights may cause him to abort the rest of the hike because the mountain has high places. The evidence, being the mountain, is real and concrete. It is therefore not false. His thoughts about the mountain (technically) are not false either in the sense that reality defined (per spiritology) is anything that is happening in the moment; therefore, reality can include the seeing of the mountain and the thinking about the mountain. But keep this in mind; thoughts are personalized realities not universal realities. This is why one man can fear to climb a mountain but another may not. Basically, whether positive or negative, thoughts are real to the individual. It is his viewpoint about the mountain that may be false because the viewer that is afraid of the mountain is also false. His viewpoint may be, "I could possibly fall," so he fears to climb. Another man that doesn't fear to climb could very well have the same viewpoint, "I could possibly fall," but he climbs anyway because of the absence of fear; he doesn't see the possibility of falling as a threat to his safety. If you tell the fearful man that the evidence is false, you could be in for quite a debate. He could bring up past accidents, news reports of land slides, loose ground, avalanches, and toppling boulders. Whoever is trying to counsel him can be in for quite a battle. However, if he looks at his viewpoint about the evidence as being false, then there may be a better chance of him disintegrating the fear because of the truthfulness of this particular assessment. The mountain is real, but the notion about the mountain's potential to harm him is false. By adopting this viewpoint, he mentally positions himself to see that it is the neurotic compulsive thinking that threatens him. So this would be the premises to begin with in order to help him overcome his fear, instead of telling him, the mountain is not real, and your mind is doctoring up imaginary ideas about an unreal object. The truth is that an unreal entity is doctoring up imaginary ideas about the real object. The spiritology acronym for fear is as follows: Faulty evaluations about reality. Even though thoughts are of the mind, they must be considered as a part of reality, and here is why. Thoughts although intangible are real. You can easily see and hear them. You can even feel them by way of emotional reactions. They don't exist on the physical realm but they do affect the physical realm. Thoughts are emissions of spiritual energy. Thoughts are the energy of creation. Think about a mountain like in the above example. It didn't always exist as you know it. It was created: fashioned and formed by the Creator. How? First the Creator thought about the mountain. It was an intangible thought, but it was real, no doubt. Therefore, the mountain was formed along with all of creation. God thought about it first, and brought it into existence by condensing His Spiritual Essence around the thought. I the writer of this piece can therefore conclude that I (personally) exist because I was (first) a thought in the mind of the creator. Through the vehicle of other created beings (my parents) I may have been conceived; they may have even wished to have a "boy," but it was the thought of the creator that formed and made me what I am today. This is why spiritology considers thoughts as reality. Thinking however can be used according to the divine design or it can be used erroneously. Therefore, thinking must be looked at and evaluated.

To evaluate something is to study it and come to a conclusion about its usefulness or worth. The man evaluates the mountain in his brain and comes to the conclusion that he should stay away from it because he has shunned heights as useless (detrimental) to his survival. He therefore fears it. In order for him to be able to climb the mountain he must be convinced that his safety is not at risk. The fearless man may not be afraid because he trusts himself and the precautions that he takes before climbing. He examines his equipment for reliability and rests upon his very own experiences of past successful climbs. The fearless climber may or may not have a true basis for being fearless. For example, it is generally understood that the law of averages is in effect. The fearless climber may overlook something and he ends up having a fall. The painful frightening experience may be stored as an emotionalized memory (trauma) and as a result, he is now afraid of heights. Both the fearful and the fearless had faulty viewpoints that were based upon their evaluations. In other words, they both evaluated the wrong thing: the wrong reality. They both based their safety on something outside of themselves or should I say something apart from themselves. The only reason a person gets afraid of anything is because he believes himself to be the wrong entity that gets afraid. The erroneous self image that sees itself apart from all (including God) is afraid. The hypnotized spirit of the individual that believes it is the false self image adopts the fear as itself. It is now afraid. Christ constantly professed, "I and the Father are One." He lived from His true spiritual essence and not from an egotistical point of view. This is why He wasn't afraid. A new and accurate evaluation must be adopted. Better said, "The truth of 'being' must be accepted." You must rediscover your spiritual nature and live from it if you ever truly hope to be fearless. The ego - your imaginary self image - the thing within (the mind) that struggles with will power, has to convince itself of having high self esteem or self confidence; the entity that debates about inadequacies or insecurities is only a product of the imagination that has taken over the life of the individual. The real spirit of the individual that is One with God cannot possibly allow thoughts or outside effects to intimidate it simply because it is a part of (One with) God, and no parts of God's Spirit or Essence could possibly be afraid. An individual must install the truth about reality in his mind, and he can only do this by knowing what the ultimate reality truly is. What is the ultimate reality? It is the unchangeable (God) Heavenly Father. Everything changes except God and His (Spirit) Spiritual nature: this is why He is eternal; if you really look at it from the scenario in this lesson, eventually, even a seemly rock solid mountain will crumble (change). Thoughts, that flow through the mind come and go (they change). A belief that is housed in the mind can also change. This includes a belief about yourself. One day you may feel that you are strong and the next day weak. This is the ebb and flow of the ego, which should be a valuable sign to you that the ego is imaginary and not real. Now contemplate this very closely: there is something that is also apart of you that hasn't changed. Over time your body has changed, your mind and its various beliefs and ideas have changed, your feelings and emotions change. However there is another element (beyond the physical, mental, and emotional) that sees and observes all the changes experienced by the entire human mechanism. This fourth and unchangeable element (the observer) is who and what you really are; it is your unchangeable spirit that is one with the Father and Christ. And because it is unchangeable, this is why it too is eternal, so there is no need to be afraid because no harm can ever come to the real you. Reevaluate your reality (understand who you really are) and become fearless through spiritology.

God is perfection and cannot create anything imperfect. This means that you were designed by God to be a perfect and fearlessly functioning being while here on the planet. Therefore you have no choice but to conclude that fear is a choice. More times than naught, it is a subconscious choice. You probably have too many fears to count. Intellectually, you know that these fears are only illusions. But you don't know that they are a product of the one illusion (ego). They trip you up, hold you back, and toss you to the four winds. Even though they are powerless illusions, you are at their mercy. Take a phobia, like the fear of heights, and if you are not afraid of heights, think about an intense fear that you have: one you wouldn't face even if your mother's life depended on it, but in the mean time, I will use the height thing as an example. This fear is capable of impeding a person's life to a great extent. I am thinking of someone at this very moment who hasn't seen family in years because of it. Now, think about the most intense fear that you believe that you have. Think about how it hampers your life. Try to recall how long you believe that you've had this fear and try to recall the first time you discovered you had it. If you can recall the first time then sit in a quiet place and with your eyes closed, repeat the recollection as best as you can from beginning to end. Try to imagine all the sights sounds smells and feelings of the event. Do this daily at least 10 to 15 minutes per sitting. If you have more time, all the better. If you can't recall the first time you ever dealt with the fear, then try to recall the last time that you know about and go from there. Now think about any lesser fears that you may have: fears that you must encounter on a daily basis. They are there and make you tense but are not overwhelming like the "heights" scenario. I'm talking about the fears that you can easily face in reality; go ahead and do so. Deliberately face the lesser fears on a daily basis and become aware of and watch the feelings and bodily reactions that accompany the feelings. Very soon, the fear will fade and your level of mental health will rise a bit.

Face as many of these minor fears as you can on a daily basis, and watch them fade into the nothingness that they are. Next, work your way up. You do this by finding the next level of fears that you feel safe to confront. Watch those fade in time as well. All the while you are doing this, you are gaining mental health and strength. The mental energy that was tied up by housing these smaller fears will be transformed into conscious energy and added strength to help dissolve the next level of fear. Those fears at the next higher level you will delightfully discover have become weaker seemly without you doing anything about them. At some point you will be able to face those intense fears that bullied you around for so long. You will be amazed also that as the lesser fears fade, this takes away strength from some of the so-called stronger fears or full blown phobias. The more of the lesser fears you abolish, the weaker the intense fears and phobias become. This is because every fear that you have has its roots in the one source that is the ego, and as you dissolve the weaker fears, you are weakening the source of your fears which takes away intensity from the more potent fears. Go ahead and face your fears starting with the weakest to the strongest, do the exercises, and watch yourself become a spiritually sound and truly confident person.

4. Be Mindful of Your Inner Dialogue:
Have you ever seen a crazy person walking down the street? I know that I have. I've seen plenty of them. The most recent that comes to mind is a man I saw standing at the corner of a very busy

intersection. He was crossing the street, back and forth. He kept pushing the pedestrian walk button and when the signal gave the go ahead, he would run across the street, stop and start yelling at an imaginary person. He was screaming and yelling and throwing punches and kicking at this make believe person. Other pedestrians where nervously avoiding and going around him. After he finished his rant, he pressed the button again, and ran to the other side from where he came; he repeated the same yelling and fighting routine. He kept doing this: going back and forth, over and over again. This is how most people live there lives. Same old maddening routines that keep them fighting with others and running back and forth while accomplishing nothing worth while. Listen to your mental conversations and compare to the crazy person on the street. You may not consider yourself crazy because you don't physically act out your maddening thoughts; but nevertheless, the insane thoughts and images are there; aren't they? In the mental world, you are no different from that crazy man on the street. Starting today, pay attention to your inner dialogue. Notice how much of it tends to be negative. Pay attention; consciously observe and listen to your inner ramblings. Even when a song gets stuck in your head, don't get frustrated; just consciously listen. This is medicine to your mindset and for your soul. Faithful and daily practice of one or more of these exercises will take you all the way to the front door of the Kingdom of Heaven, and Christ Himself will open the door and let you in, so don't hesitate. Get Started, and Godspeed!

Book VI Reflections:
1. Whenever you decide to pray, pray with self awareness.
2. Notice how labels are coveted and believed in by yourself and others
3. Say truth based affirmations while noticing the discomfort that arises.
4. Each time you meet fear head on with conscious awareness you diminish it.
5. Practice one or more of the fear ridding techniques on a daily basis.

Book VII:

The State of Man:

Man is lost. He doesn't know who he is but is caught up in an illusion that he knows himself. He is hypnotized. He believes that in the grand scheme of things that his frantic chasings and lifestyle give real meaning to his existence: careers, marriage, family are just a few of the devices that man has deluded himself with in order to extract meaning from his life. It is all illusion. It is idol worship. Man was once cast out of the Garden of Eden: removed from the Grace of God. Henceforth, his identity was lost; man desperately craves an identity, so he acquired an artificial one. He created the ego. Man needs to feel and believe that he is somebody special. He craves a sense of importance, and the artificial id gave him that sense of being someone special and important. The flaw that came with this false id is a sense of separation from God and his fellow man. This sense of separation is the cause of all his misery, mayhem, and destruction. Because he believes he is separate from his fellow man, he compares himself with his fellow man. He then believes himself to be inferior or superior by comparison. Even if he believes that he has met someone that he has found something in common with and then joins the other in an attempt at unification, he still compares himself even with his so called ally. This also occurs with relationships he has with the opposite sex. Because of the false sense of superiority and inferiority, he resents, hates, or even wars with his fellow man. Worst of all, he wars with himself and doesn't know it. His ego/false self is his downfall. This is the state of man, and his ego is the only problem that needs to be remedied. If mankind were to abolish the false id and become reconciled to God in spirit, then all other problems: mental illness, in many cases physical sickness, famine, war, crime, etc... would cease to exist. A man cannot alter the state of the world, but he is always attempting to do so without realizing how futile his efforts are; a man can only correct his own internal state. Self correction is the only answer for this troubled world, and each individual must take it upon himself to accomplish this worthy task for it is the only way to get back to Paradise.

This I know:

I know the struggles and victories of this journey (of ego dissolution) that you are about to embark upon.

I know the frustration that you will encounter whenever your progress seems slow or stalled.

I know about the times that you will try to tell your closest friends and family about your newfound path, and they will reject you. They will tell you that their own systems, the very systems (organized religions and other cults) that you used to be a part of, are the correct way. Just keep moving forward. Live your life. Don't worry about having to tell others. That will come in its own time and in its own way. That particular decision isn't yours to make anyway; God will decide that for you. Don't try to make anything happen. Just flow with the journey. The beauty of this system is that you don't have to quit being a Christian or Muslim or Buddhist or whatever else you are a part of. You don't have to make any drastic changes or commitments. How wonderful is that?

I know about the multiple occasions whenever you will seemed to have regressed or moved backwards; trust me, on the spiritual path, there is no regression.

I know about the changes that will happen to you and in your life without you totally understanding why: people that you've associated with for years or even been in relationships with (boyfriends, girlfriends, even spouses) may go away for no apparent reason. This is because their level of mental maturity no longer matches your own, and as they go, others will appear, and depending on the speed of your growth, those new people will also go away and be replaced by others. This will happen especially if those people are not on the same spiritual journey with the ultimate goal being total dissolution of the ego. You yourself will even decide to stop associating with certain people. Don't let this bother you. It is part of the process. This I know.

I know about the times you'll spend all alone which are the most valuable times. The time spent alone can be used to study and get acquainted with yourself by looking at and ultimately abolishing the feeling of loneliness once and for all.

I know about the times you will forget your spiritual exercises for days, even months at a time, and fall back into spiritual sleep, but don't be concerned with it. You never left the path and are still making progress because you've already planted the good seeds of truth.

I know about the times that even though you know you've made progress, the imaginary ego will present convincing arguments to keep itself alive (all of them along the lines of "What's the use? You're wasting your time. It's all futility and nonsense. The ego can never completely go away"). Don't listen to it. Just sit back, relax, and allow the Spirit to finish clearing and cleansing your mind. There will be times that you think you've reached a milestone and or conquered a certain fear only to have it resurface in an effort to discourage you from the path. Don't buy into it. You are making progress.

I also know about the distant unconscious and long forgotten memories that will resurface to your conscious awareness. Some will be pleasant and some won't. Your job will be to not relish them or cringe from them but to silently observe them as they surface and watch them fade away back into the subconscious. I'm sure you've heard declarations like, "Everytime you take a step towards God, God takes a step towards you." I assure you that this is true.

I know about the times you will think or your imaginary ego will try to convince you (to keep its imaginary existence in tact, of course) that you are working all alone without help from Above. Just ignore it, and you will eventually understand that you are not and never was alone.

I know that new fears will pop up: fears that you never even knew you had will suddenly appear before you, or things that have never frightened you before, you will be afraid of. You can rest easy though. This is a trick of the ego and a sign of its most intense desperation to scare you into returning to itself. It will invent countless and all kinds of negativities, forebodings, and illusions that you must calmly ignore.

I know about the self-righteous arguments you will waste your time in: trying to get people to correct themselves and you will have to resolve to not waste your precious time and energy on this. These people cannot as of yet see beyond their egos. Although it appears that you are on the same page of understanding, they will not really know what you are talking about, and you risk driving them deeper into spiritual sleep. Do your best to leave this alone and let the way you live your life do the talking for you.

I know about the moments of clarity you will experience and get excited over only to be followed by periods of mental agitation and chaos (up and down like a rollercoaster, in and out like the ocean tide). Keep in mind that the spiritual road has smooth places and rough spots with potholes; never mind that, just rest assured that you will never run off the road into a ditch; God Himself will not allow this to happen.

I know about the halfway point. It is that point when the Spirit and your imaginary ego will be in a tug of war battle for supremacy. Back and forth your consciousness will go from present moment awareness to mental absorption (even on a daily basis). At this point you can rejoice because the battle has been (always was) won.

I know about the good things you will experience: the gradual rise in mental well being, memory improvement, more enthusiasm and zest for life, the gradual decline of fear and negativity, the gradual rise in patience and understanding, moments of mental clarity quietness and peace, the comments that you'll receive from people like, "there's something different about you." the way your relations with people will be more pleasant and positive, the way you will gradually become more decisive, constructive, and productive.

I know about the possible physical changes: allergies reduced or eliminated, (the author was able to throw away an asthma inhaler that was a crutch since childhood) physical body feeling lighter and more nimble, reflex improvements, I cannot really say what will happen to you on a physical level since I don't know your condition, but I can say that improvements will more than likely happen. The physical always follow suit with the mental.

Finally, I know that your persistence and endurance will pay off huge dividends, so keep moving ahead until that magical day happens, and at last, you enter the Kingdom of Heaven.

Whenever you feel discouraged or downtrodden, read the "This I know" section.

Something else you should know:

If you are faithfully committed to the dissolution of the false self, there will come a time when you have achieved a considerable amount of mental and spiritual elevation but are still battling with the same old negative habits and mental struggles.

You will be able to see, feel, and get practical benefits from the goodness while simultaneously grappling with the badness.

This is because the ego is still there, although to a lesser degree, playing its same old games and nonsense. It's a compulsive, mechanical, and reactionary thing; it knows no other way to operate. It will fight for its existence until the very end. Don't worry about it, just continue with your program of spiritual self improvement and ignore the ego as best as you can. Remember the example of the glass of pure water: Throw a handful of dirt (faulty beliefs, untruths, useless labels) in a glass of pure water (a naive mind) and you get muddy water (ego/false self). This water is useless and undrinkable. However, if you start the filtering process, (self observation) the water gradually becomes clearer. You can see it with your own eyes as it clears up, but you can also see that there is still more purification to be done, and the water is not yet drinkable. Keep up with purification process and at some point, the final grain of dirt will be removed. Now you have pure and clean water (the kingdom of God) that you can drink; this pure water renews you and refreshes your entire system and the good news is that you can never be corrupted again, but remember, you can't do anything with the water until that last grain of dirt (erroneous concepts) is removed. Also remember, that it is totally possible to remove all the dirty filth of the ego. Don't let it talk you into believing that this is an impossible task.

You will know that your power of consciousness has increased, and it should be easier for you...

to not cower in certain circumstances

to swallow foolish pride

to remain silent when need be

to not react in anger

to resist the urge to fawn in front of people you consider impressive in some way (idol worship) to speak up whenever you need to say something

to not be judgmental of people

to attempt to understand people instead of being upset with them.

You will know that you have extra power and can consciously do battle (by impartial observation) resulting in a speedier end of the ego; this equates to resisting its urges and promptings just like Christ did when he confronted satan in the wilderness.

A quick word about Self Esteem and Self Confidence:

Self Esteem and Self Confidence as you currently know them are both a myth. They are twins of deception: vanity and illusion. The reason is because they are both tied up in your imagination about what you think you are and what you have been brainwashed into believing you should be; they are a product of your ego/false self. Remember, the ego self is all about separation from God and duality; it can only compare inner and outer circumstances to itself. This explains why some days you are more confident than others. You can speak up with friends and family but are scared to death to speak before an audience of strangers. One day you are unstoppable and on top of the world. The next day, you can barely drag yourself out of bed. One day you tell your significant other that your love knows no limits; the next day you indignantly scream about being disrespected or a pet peeve being violated, and you don't speak to him or her for days or maybe you call off the relationship. I know; I know. You're probably thinking, "Well, I am a confident person with high self esteem, but I'm also human. See? This is a typical egotistical answer (cop out).

This type of artificial confidence is of the ego and waivers back and forth depending on your mental associations of what is happening inside and outside of you. You use the ego to conjure it up. It is the phony confidence that is used to do battle with or deal with a person or circumstance that is perceived as a separate entity or obstacle.

Real confidence that is of a spiritual nature doesn't see things in terms of separate entities and obstacles. It knows that all is one with God (as Christ constantly proclaimed) and therefore knows that God will handle the situation in a way that is best for all. Real confidence and self esteem are not products of the ego. The only way to achieve them is to banish the false self by getting outside of your mind thereby doing away with the imaginary self image. Once achieved, you are in the present moment, the Kingdom of Heaven, the true here and now. This is where true confidence and self esteem dwell. If you really want either one of them, in truth, they are one and the same, then you too must abide in the present moment: in this place you merely rest in confidence and self esteem without even thinking about it. In this place, confidence never waivers back and forth, nor does self esteem falter. You can only achieve the real by seeing that what you have now is false. As Christ once said, "You remain blind because you claim to have sight."

Don't be afraid to question the religious zealots:

You have every right to do so because it is your soul that is at stake; don't let faithless religious hypocrites steal your soul by conning you into believing that it is disrespectful or blasphemous to question anything. They have given away their own souls and are now on the side of evil. Their mission and sole purpose is to collect and send as many souls as possible to hell, and they don't even know it. These soulless hollow human beings will try to manipulate and control you for the sake of ego gratification. Be mindful of this subtle form of cruelty. Whenever they try to preach to you about faith in God, ask them about their own faith; of course they will tell you that their faith is strong and unshakeable and this is your cue to ask for a demonstration. They will not want to comply or they may come up with some testimonial from their past like being cured of an illness to try and sway you. Don't go for it. Ask them to demonstrate in the here and now. This goes for preachers, pastors, ministers, and so-called prophets. They will think of all sorts of reasons and evasions to get themselves off the hook. You will know they are faithless by their instant reactions of anxiousness, defensiveness, and indignation. The general attitude is how dare you question my ethics or are you calling me a liar? Yes you are because they are liars. They may even try to make you feel ashamed and guilty for asking. Don't back down. They will try to give you the Biblical story of when Jesus told Thomas, "you believe because you have seen; blessed are those that have not seen but believe anyway." Don't go for it. If it was wrong for Thomas to want to see, then Jesus would not have let him put his fingers in the wounds. Remember, Jesus walked throughout the land giving demonstrations because He knew that seeing is believing. He knew that demonstration was the only way to bring people to the Kingdom. Question them all. Ask for an immediate demonstration. Tell them that God requires you to question and ask for demonstrations. Remind them of a few facts:

Moses demonstrated his faith by demonstrating the Power of God to Pharaoh and the people of Egypt and Israel. God required the demonstrations simply because people are skeptical from being under the devil's influence. Even people with common sense simply will not believe unless they see and experience something for themselves. Nothing has changed. God is still the same as He was yesterday and years past, and God still requires demonstrations. Remember, faith without works (demonstrations) is dead!

Prophets are no longer needed:

A word to Christianity about prophets: truly they are no longer needed. Christ the Savior was the alpha and omega, the first authority and final prophet, teacher, minister, demonstrator (Son of God) for the redemption of mankind. Most of the modern day prophets that you follow are all deceivers. I know that you are desperate for someone to believe in, but at some point, it is inevitable that you stop trusting in men and turn to God. The problem is that the ego must have something physical or tangible to base its belief upon. It is because of the sense of separation that it harbors. It keeps itself in tact by putting trust in other false egos. To look within and find God would mean its destruction. You say that you've accepted Christ, but you cling to these charlatans in hopes that they can provide you with something that will give you peace of mind and hope for prosperity. These fakers speak to you in vague generalizations and continue to drain your pocket book. These hypocrites tell you to have faith, but fail to demonstrate real faith in their rants. If they were real prophets, then their own faith would be sufficient. Did the pharaoh believe Moses? Did Thomas believe that it was really Jesus standing before him after the crucifixion? The answer to both these questions is no. They did not have the faith; however, both Christ and Moses presented demonstrations to these unbelievers, after which, they believed. See these false prophets for what they really are. Don't let them tell you that they cannot provide a demonstration because your faith is weak. If they were real, then your faith wouldn't matter; their very own faith would be enough. As long as you keep depending on them, you have no hope of finding God. Think about it. If you've truly accepted Christ, then what could you possibly need a replacement or supplemental prophet for? Guidance? No way; if you've truly accepted Christ, then the comforter would have come, and with it comes guidance and insight. With the acceptance of salvation, comes the automatic guidance of God. They can't predict the future anyway. Is this what you are hoping for? Confirmation that everything will be ok in the future? Those that truly have unconditional faith in God do not need to know, nor do they worry about what the future holds. It doesn't matter to the truly faithful how tumultuous, violent, corrupt, and uncertain the world is. Those that have accepted Christ have become unified with the Father, Son, and Holy Spirit; they're spiritually secure and mentally sound. With this unification comes the knowing of what is in store (at hand even): the Kingdom of Heaven. Those that have truly accepted have no need for a prophet in their lives. Christ was the final and permanent authority on Salvation. Looking to these con-artists for help is to deny Christ and God. You will eventually have to let go of dependence upon all men anyway before God will finally reveal Himself to you because dependence on another human equates to idol worship. You can start by dismissing these representatives of the devil. Get away from these false prophets while there is still time to save your soul; consciously endure the uncertainty and anxiety that comes after you've dismissed all false sources of guidance and the Real Comforter will come.

About Public Speaking:

Do you have a fear of public speaking? A great number of people struggle with this most common phobia. This is one of the more interesting of them all because of the mystery behind it. It's mysterious because of its vagueness. Many people just don't understand why they have this fear. There are some exceptions, but I am speaking about normal people that can easily talk to friends and family even in environments where there are multiple people listening. It's hard to figure out mainly because in theory, most people shouldn't suffer from this fear (they have no trauma to justify the fear). Many people can't tell where it comes from and some people have a history of speaking in front of crowds, even as a kid, and they still continue to suffer. So why are so many people afflicted with this puzzling condition? It's time for a new theory. We've already touched upon the ego and how it is responsible for so much of our life's misery and turmoil. This condition is no different. It too is ego generated, so we will add it to the list. We also talked about how awareness, conscious seeing, of the ego and what it does is the way to freedom. Ok, so the ego doesn't like to be paid attention to. When it feels that it's being watched, it knows that it may possibly be detected, found out, and finally seen as the imaginary fraud that it is. If that happens then it will start to unravel and dissolve. It thinks that it is a real entity and doesn't want to die, so it shrieks, squirms, panics, and starts to shake you up. It is literally telling you, "Noooo, please don't kill me! Don't do it! Get out before it's too late!" Since you believe that you are this fake entity, you translate its pain and panic to yourself. Now you think that you are going to die or go through whatever kind of other pain your ego has associated to being watched. In the relaxed atmospheres when you are telling a joke to your guests at a party, there is usually no sense of being paid attention to so the ego believes it is safe and is quite comfortable in these surroundings; however, in the more formal environments, you can pretty much guess, there is an intense feeling of being paid attention to isn't there? It starts with all the people in front of you looking at you with those hostile glares. Yes, the ego considers all attention to itself has being hostile. This in turn causes you to look inward and at yourself, and lets face it, taking a good long look at yourself is what causes the ego to lose its pseudo power over you. However, the ego will give you all kinds of surface reasons to throw you off of its scent: am I dressed properly, I must look like an idiot up here, etc... so that being said, public speaking can be a major weapon in shattering the ego to a million pieces if you look at yourself consciously while you are shaking up in front of the audience. This shaking up process is the ego being unraveled.

Do the thing you fear and death of fear is certain:

You've heard this cliché before; I'm sure, but I found out the hard way that it's not necessarily true. You can perform an act that you're afraid to do a thousand or more times, but if you habitually and mechanically become self absorbed in the fearful emotion, then you are just spinning your wheels, and the fear may even intensify; however, doing the thing you fear while being aware that you are afraid will be the certain death of fear.

About Love:

Love is completely unselfish and not many people know what true love really is. Just about everyone you know is selfish to some degree. To love something is to thoroughly understand it and not necessarily have feelings of sentimentality for it. To really understand love is to implement it: it is an internally operating fact that is second nature and not just head knowledge. We all know from visible evidence that there aren't many who are completely unselfish. The number one reason why most don't know love is because they don't truly understand love, although they may think they understand because of a memorized definition. The average has ego love or human love. The ego/false self has invented its own personalized meaning of love in order to support its sinister agenda of keeping itself alive and keeping you in spiritual bondage. If someone says something like, "If you love me, then you will_____." You fill in the blank. This is that person's ego trying to manipulate or demand, and love doesn't do either. Let's face it. Most people are not capable of real love because they house a selfish ego but desperately need to believe that they are loving, so what they do is conjure up artificiality (also sentimental feelings) and call it love. They buy into this lie and false definition then pretend to each other that all is well. They want to be selfish and self-centered and at the same time loving which is an impossible feat. In order to achieve this double standard, the real meaning has to be twisted and distorted. Having altered the meaning, the ego now gets its way and is able to use, abuse, and mislead others all the while telling the victims, "I love you or I am doing this for your own good." This is why it is often said that we tend to hurt the ones we love most. Real love doesn't know pain. It doesn't hurt anyone or allow itself to be hurt. The ego will make all sorts of excuses to keep false love alive: excuses like, if I am totally unselfish, then people will use and take advantage of me; I'd rather have it the other way around; better the victor than the victim. You don't have to buy into this lie either, because real love also includes self-love and a truly loving person not only loves others, but loves himself, and will not allow the other to use or abuse him. The truly loving realizes that if he allows another to take advantage, then he is cooperating with that person's evilness and thereby risking both their souls being cast into hell. Because the wrong meaning of love is harbored in the mind is the chief reason why most don't enter the Kingdom. This is the last hurdle to leap over: admitting that one doesn't know what love really is even though they have the definition memorized. The ego adamantly refuses to admit that it doesn't know. It doesn't want to be exposed as a fraud. As said before, its biggest fear is exposure. Ironically, exposure is the only cure. Once it is the detected by its host, it begins to die. Ego detection and ejection is all that is necessary to become a truly loving person.

Synonyms to keep in mind:

Awareness = freedom = consciousness = dwelling in the present moment = understanding = wisdom = courage = flexibility = calmness = happiness = faith = taking no thought for tomorrow = goodness = perfection = godliness = spirituality = peace = salvation = The Kingdom of Heaven

Ego = bondage = unconsciousness = inverted awareness = living in a doctored up past, pseudo present or vague and uncertain future = the devil = folly = confidence = living from negative imagination = self image = self esteem = contrariness = stubbornness = will power = belief = sin = anxiety = worry = uncertainty = doubt = fear = futility = the kingdom of hell.

See if you can come up with some of your own.

The difference between:

The difference between confidence and courage:
Confidence is the suppression of fear. Courage is the absence of fear. The confident person struggles and wrestles to subdue fear so that he may deal with a crisis. The courageous person rests in the arms of his fearless nature and allows the crisis to be dealt with by God.

The difference between faith and belief:

The bible says that faith is the evidence of things unseen. This is true; however, it springs from an inner knowing. Faith is rock solid knowing which is beyond a mere belief or conviction. Faith can never be wrong. It is based upon reality. There is never any uncertainty involved. The person with faith does not err. The person with faith is calm and unmoved. God would never throw you to the wolves and say, "just trust Me." He provides you with the fearless capacity to trust and endure whatever storm is raging around you.

Belief is a mental certainty that may or may not even be true. Even if it is true, such as a belief that God exists, it can have a foundation of doubt or be based purely on imagination and hearsay. A believer may believe, but he may not know. The person who believes is anxious and nervous. It is the devil that puts you in hardships and then tells you that this is a test from God. The evidence of this being the devil's work is the anxiety, worry, fear, or any other negative state that accompanies you while you are trying to cope. Faith is spiritual awareness (absolute knowing).

Yes, the believer believes, but the faithful knows. The ultimate difference between faith and courage vs. confidence and belief is that the first is the result of awareness while the latter is a product of the ego. I describe my living room to you and you believe what I tell you; you come to my house and sit in my living room and now you are aware without trying to believe. Try and see the difference. This is how you must come to know God.

Spiritology Proverbs
Godly vs. egotistical:

The godly is one in a million and truly knows God. The egotistical is one of a million and knows a self created concept of God.

The egotistical invites others to church and then takes credit for leading them to salvation.

The godly allows others to approach and explains to them that they (themselves) are responsible for petitioning God for deliverance.

Ask the egotistical if he knows God and you'll get a loud resounding "Yes! I am strong in the Lord!" Ask the same question to the godly and you will receive a slight but serene smile.

The egotistical is trustful in the goodness of human nature; the godly trust only in the benevolence of the Lord.

The egotistical has thousands of worries about the future; the godly has no concern whatsoever as to the unfolding of his life.

The egotistical struggles feverishly to stay afloat by treading water; the godly rests comfortably inside the boat calmly knowing that he won't even get wet.

A tree is known by the fruit it bears; hence the godly can never be agitated nor can the egotistical cease to be frantic.

Never ending nervousness incessantly plagues the egotistical while continuous contentment follows the godly.

On a daily basis, the godly reaps the blessings of his personality while the egotistical suffers the torment of his.

On the last day, the godly's character will be his reward, as will the egotistical's nature result in his punishment.

The paradox of spiritual growth:

To grow you must shrink. I'll repeat it a little differently; to grow spiritually, you must shrink psychologically. This is an old concept. You must clear out or get rid of the old in order to make way for the new. You must replace your ego by gradually and systematically reducing it until it completely vanishes. It is this reduction that nurtures the growth. If this is done, then you will find that spiritual growth happens simultaneously of its own accord to the extent that you reduce the ego. Like two ships passing in the night, each going in opposite directions, as the ego shrinks, awareness expands. Want to be void of fear and worldly problems? Of course you do. That is the "real you" does. The ego doesn't because it would mean riddance to its imaginary existence; it is the sole cause of all problems and tragedies of the human condition. The ego's identity is tied up into these problems, so it cannot bear to have you lose them. Not only that, but the ego has all kinds of sinister tricks and lies so that its existence which is your misery will remain. One of its diabolical hoaxes is giving you false solutions to your worldly problems: like replacing a spouse that you're no longer compatible with. The truth of the matter is that, no matter what, two individuals dwelling in ego possession will ultimately clash. Another trick is to tell you that this world is a bad place, but you yourself, although not perfect, are doing the best you can; therefore, you are not part of the problem. It is always other people and organizations at fault. To really see and not justify your errors is the end of the ego.

Another form of deception is to convince you that you can't live without it. Most people believe it. Some will think, "If I lose my ego then what will I become or who will I be?" Don't worry about who or what you will be. Just take a leap of faith and expel the ego. Others will reason, "If I banish my ego, then I will be and have nothing." Dismiss this line of false logic. The truth is that if you get rid of the ego then you will be and have everything (salvation).

By far the most evil game that it plays is the game of identity theft. It has stolen your identity, and now you believe that you are your ego. You think that you are your imagination. You must see that the ego is nothing but imagination: your self created self-image. This self image that you've invented has a domino effect that results in the perpetual ruining of your life. It is this pseudo self that tricks you into needing validation from others and tells you that you must have strong self esteem (which by the way will never happen). What you think is strong self esteem is merely the suppression of insecurity, but the ego won't tell you that. This is why most miss the mark of spiritual growth. Their idea of spiritual growth is tied up into egotism and its false data about having high self esteem and strong self confidence. The key being the word "self." The ego is always thinking about itself and everything it encounters draws to it some kind of self reference. A spiritually grown person is aware of himself but does not indulge in mental self reference.

Book VII Reflections:

1. Man is hypnotized (spiritually asleep). This is the only cause of all his troubles.
2. Flow with your spiritual journey without trying to make anything happen.
3. See that what you now have is false (ego), and you will possess the Real (God).
4. See that fear and (emotional) pain are the exact same thing.
5. Don't be bluffed by religious zealots. God requires you to question (test) them all. Remember, "Faith without works (demonstrations) is dead. Talking and preaching doesn't translate into faith.
6. Tell yourself the truth about yourself for the sake of spiritual healing.
7. Prophets are no longer needed since Christ came. Remember His last words from the cross, "It is finished!"
8. Fear of public speaking is your ego/false self not wanting to draw attention to itself or be seen for what it really is: a fake.
9. Do the thing you fear and death of fear is certain if done with awareness.
10. Keep in mind the difference between awareness and the ego.
11. Try and understand that confidence and courage are not the same thing.
12. See that belief and faith can be different.
13. Consider that spiritual growth is a paradox: you grow your "Self" by self reduction.
14. Recognize all the tricks and games that the ego plays to keep itself alive.

15. A spiritual grownup has no egotistical self references.
16. Review the synonyms.

Book VIII

God is Real:

Yes, you say, "God is Real," but it is only lip service. You know only the pseudo real: the fake real. You believe that you know God, but in reality, you know (and serve) the devil. To know God is to constantly commune and not waiver. You dwell in the bosom of the devil, and to truly know God, you must confess that you don't. (another reminder) Didn't Jesus Himself say, "It is because you claim to have sight, that you remain blind?" You must try to understand the spiritual message behind this verse. Admit that you don't know God and eventually you will truly be able to exclaim, "God is Real!" This is because the devil's bluff (ego version of what God is) will be what you are truly denying. The instant you deny the devil is the very instant that you accept God and give Him permission to instill His True Self into your mind and heart. You will then cease to commune with the devil and will know that God is Real.

I AM:

I AM the Father, Son, and Holy Ghost.
I AM Omnipotent, Omniscient, and Omnipresent.
I AM the Way, Truth, and the Life.
I AM the Mental, Physical, and Spiritual.
I AM the First and the Last.
I AM the Alpha and Omega: the Beginning and the End.

I AM without beginning and without end: the end without beginning and beginning without end.
I AM Infinite, Eternal, and Universal.
I AM the Creator and the Creation.
I AM Everything seen and unseen.
I AM the quiet and the storm.
I AM all substance and law.
I AM the Lord.
I AM Christ.
I AM You (all of you) and you are ME (part of me). We are One and the same.
I AM within you, and you are within ME. We Are One. I complete you, and you complete Me. We are One (Since I cannot die, neither can you: physical bodies come and go, they change, but We remain eternal).
Do not try to imagine or envision Who or What I AM for that is establishing a graven image and idol worship.
I AM beyond human identification.
I AM the Universal Almighty and cannot be boxed or housed within your limited intellects and imaginations.
I AM the Lord your God, and to envision Me is too look upon the devil.
I AM the Supreme Spirit, and I have no adversaries or enemies.
I AM All and I have no opposition or competition.
I AM Everything and I have no favorites.
I AM Everyone, and no one is favored beyond anyone else in MY Eyes.
I AM The Holy One, and all are equal because all belong to Me.

I AM your Father. See that your relationship with Me is truly one sided and needs to be reconciled and your salvation is assured.

I AM your Protector. Cease your internal fighting and resistance.

I AM your Salvation, and You must truly realize that the war is over: the battle has been won: even before the beginning of time. Yes, even the angels are at rest.

I AM Victory; for those who truly know me, there is no defeat.

I AM Limitless; cease all vain attempts to apply your human attributes to Me.

I AM without flaw; cease identifying yourselves with imperfection (the devil).

I AM Perfect: Perfection.

I AM not capable of imperfection, nor can anything I create be imperfect.

I AM without barriers or errors; use your God given reason; how can the All Powerful and Perfect One create anything of imperfection.

Cease all vain attempts at finding meaning and purpose for your lives, for I AM your life; therefore, finding and uniting yourself with Me is your life's sole purpose.

I AM all that you need. Searching for happiness and contentment in exterior things (family, marriage, friendships, material possessions, money, power, fame) will only lead you deeper into the desert of despair (kingdom of hell) and away from True Happiness and Contentment that is the Kingdom of Heaven. These exterior items are secondary and should be put in their proper place; for as my Son, Christ, said, "Seek first the Kingdom of Heaven and its righteousness, and all other things (secondary) will be added unto you."

Hearken unto Me:

I once told you to be fruitful and multiply. Be prosperous in life and have it more abundantly, but don't allow the devil to confuse My material and worldly gifts to you with your true purpose for existing: which is union and fellowship with Me. Neither I nor Christ told you to go out and form separate religious sects. Examine the results of this grave error (war, division, debauchery, perversion) and make right the wrongs that you've perpetrated by way of the devil in My Holy Name. You must acquire a new meaning for the word "evil."
The wars, murders, countless varieties of crime, brother against brother, country vs. country, religions opposing each other and foolishly claiming Me as their own: This is all nonsense (foolish pride, folly, and vanity). This is not the evil; these are actions, (exterior) results, and byproducts of evil. The true evil is the ego that keeps you imprisoned in spiritual sleep. That is what evil is. Evil is the opposite of "live." Evil is inverted living. To be asleep is the opposite of being awake, and a spiritually awake individual cannot perpetrate the actions of a sleeping one. To truly see evil is to see that you are asleep, and the seeing will prompt awakening which in turn destroys evil.

Spritology Proverbs:

Christ vs. Organized Christianity:

Christ is Truth.
Organized Christianity is hypocrisy.

Christ is Reality.
Organized Christianity is delusion.

Christ is the Light of the world.
Organized Christianity is the spiritual veil.

Christ is One, Whole, and Complete.
Organized Christianity is many, divided, and fragmented.

Christ is the Real and Nameless One (I AM).
Organized Christianity is false identification.

Christ is the way to salvation.
Organized Christianity leads away from Paradise to hell.

Christ is Everything you need and All you desire.
Organized Christianity can offer only pain and suffering.

Christ is Real Security for those who truly know Him.
Organized Christianity is nervous doubt and trembling to its members.

Christ has already redeemed His people once and for all.
Organized Christianity offers salvation repetitiously without responsibility for sin.

Christ is forever and so are those who truly know Him.
Organized Christianity is temporal and will be forgotten in the end time.

Normal vs. Natural:

The devil is normal.
God is Natural.

Fear is normal.
Courage is natural.

The ego is a normal but false existence.
Detached awareness is natural living.

Emotionalization of labels is normal.
Non identification is natural.

Nervousness in pressure situations is perfectly normal.
To remain calm under the same circumstances is natural.

Frustration is the normal response when desire is thwarted.
Contentment is the natural result whether or not desire is fulfilled.

Belief is normal.
Faith (knowing) is natural.

Repressed evil calls itself goodness and is
considered normal.
True goodness inside and out is natural.

A depressed man thinks that his depression is
justifiable and normal.
A truly happy man knows that his happiness is a
natural state that is beyond any justification,
exterior circumstance, or explanation.

Anger is a normal reaction that can eventually ruin
a man's life.
Peace is a natural reaction that enhances the
individual and his world.

To wallow in defeat is normal.
To immerge victorious is natural.

Lying is normal.
Honesty is natural.

The devil's destruction is normal.
The Salvation of God is natural.

Falling for the devil's trickery is normal.
Yielding to the Truth of God is natural.

Power of choice:

I gave you the power of choice, and your first
choice was to misuse it.

You misused it by giving it away.
You first decided to enthrone a false god (the devil) in my place.
Afterwards, you foolishly relinquished that power over to the devil (giving him the right to choose for you).
Next, you became his obedient, mechanical, reactionary minion.
He made you do foolish things for his own twisted pleasure.
He told you lies, and you accepted those lies.
His first lie to you was that you belong to him.
He then tricked you into believing that you and he are one (your ego = your spirit).
Next, he convinced you that I have no connection to you, and told you to deny this fact but lie to yourself and everyone else that all is well.
He caused you to believe that I exist somewhere outside of you: somewhere distant and far off.
He told you to memorize scripture and vainly repeat it to each other but at the same time live a self centered lifestyle.
He convinced you that hypocrisy is acceptable to Me.
He told you that you'd never meet Me (experience My Salvation) until you die (experience physical death).
Because of his lies, you believe that the salvation of the Lord is like a myth or fairy tale which is why you behave like scoundrels. You basically do not believe in Me.
He caused you to think that you are different (inferior to or superior to) your fellow brethren.
He caused you to resent and hate each other.

He told you that you must conquer and enslave one another.
He told you that your survival depends upon your brother's demise.
You murder your fellow man because of his lies.
He convinced you that you won't have anything of value unless you take it by force.
You listened to him when he told you to beat and humiliate your child.
You honored his request when he told you to commit infidelity.
Without any compassion, you went ahead and abandoned your family upon his order.
He convinced you (your ancestors) to betray and crucify Christ.
To this day he is still influencing you to dishonor and take for granted Christ's ultimate sacrifice.
He tells you to accept the salvation of Christ, not because you truly believe, but because everyone else is doing it and you shouldn't be a social outcast.
He told you to ignore the still small voice within that urges you to do the right thing.
Even now, he tells you that to have a relationship with the One True God requires that you sacrifice your current happiness and way of life which is miserable.
He fooled you into believing that acceptance of misery is the only way to live.
You accept everything he tells you but intellectually claim that he doesn't influence you.
Yet and still, there is a small amount of power (choice) left in you that the devil cannot touch.
Will you use it wisely?

Will you use it to take back your original power and get your Life back?
Will you use it and come back to Me?

What is God doing?

Some would say that God is busy being the glue that holds the universe together. He's busy keeping the planets rotating in orbit, busy growing the flowers and trees, busy keeping your blood circulating and renewing your physical body, busy keeping the sun shining and the ocean tides coming in and going out, busy coordinating the cycle of birth and death on a cellular level, earthly level, and planetary level. Humans often provide assists with the death part on an earthly level, but they are still a product of God's wisdom and part of His ultimate plan even though it doesn't appear as such. In other words, God is busy with up keeping and maintaining all of creation. Since this is so, some reason that God doesn't dibble and dabble (intervene or interfere) in human affairs. This is conditionally true to an extent. He gives you the power of choice. The confusion comes because humans try to do everything in their own way and on their own terms. Everything is about egotistical self reference. They want to deal with God as they would handle another human being. Even in their misery, they are so conceited that they believe they can petition God according to human standards and rules. The game of Life is real, and man cannot make up the rules. God established His laws even before the sun was formed. God doesn't intervene because humans use their power of choice to thwart Him. God is hinting, "Until you truly choose Me, I cannot help you." Even if you subconsciously choose evil, God would be a devilish tyrant if He violated your power of choice. Devout religious folk will disagree, but there can be no denying of the constant doing and thinking bad about themselves, other people, and the world around them. Yes, you are choosing to think negative and evil thoughts. This choice seems to be of an automatic and subconscious nature, but in reality, it is because you fear to give up the ego. People even choose to idolize other humans (athletes, religious and world leaders, etc) by putting them on God's level. They think to themselves and even teach their children to be like these individuals. No! You must be Christlike and that is all there is to it. To teach your children otherwise is to foster egotism. People think and behave badly toward life and turn around and ask God for forgiveness and divine intervention, and they secretly know in their minds (all the while praying) that they will immediately revert back to their (false) sinful natures. That is not real praying. Christ said, "I have not come to do away with the law but to see that it is fulfilled." Think and behave badly and the law will execute judgment upon you. Sometimes it may seem like you get away with exterior bad behavior, but it will eventually boomerang upon you. However, the punishment for interior bad behavior (negative thinking) is usually immediate. Fear, anger, depression, anxiety, etc... are all the result of immediate punishment by the law for thinking badly. People will ask equally and sometimes weaker religious leaders to pray and petition for them to no avail. Keep in mind that faithless prayers have potentially negative consequences that can result in what Job exclaimed, "The thing that I feared most has come upon me." Indeed it is better to not pray than to utter a faithless prayer. People pray in one moment, and in the next, they go back to doing and thinking badly. This is an evil, repetitious, and mechanical cycle that humans refuse to recognize. They are unaware and do not know that recognition must go beyond intellectual recognition. Humans must become consciously aware. That is all that needs to be done. Verbalizing thoughts in the form of begging and pleading and calling it "prayer" is not the way. That is the human way, not God's way. You don't have to beg God; just trust Him. Initially, you can start by using your intellect to honestly and unemotionally see and admit that you don't know the difference between intellectual knowing and true awareness. This is how you ignite the fire that eventually starts the process of melting away the ego thereby allowing God to come to your rescue. Once the ego is gone, so goes the devil, and so goes all of your troubles and turmoil; once the ego is out, God remains. Divine intervention (constant incessant communion with God) becomes your way of life. The devil is no longer manipulating you like a puppet because God is now in control based upon the fact that you gave Him your permission on His terms. The reason for all earthly tragedies and nonsense is because humans refuse to give up their egos (the devil). They even teach their innocent children to accept and develop a separate ego (devil). Humans refuse to see that doing things the egotistical way results in tragic dead ends. They stubbornly continue to think that they can keep their egos in tact and be at one (commune) with God. If you have an ego, while you were in church believing you were communing with and praying to God, you were actually cohabitating and cooperating with the devil. To possess an ego, even one that considers itself humble and behaves in noble benevolent ways, means separation, and separation always invites tragedy into the ego possessed person's life. It is the devil wedging himself between you and God. God cannot abide with the devil. God will not abide with the devil, and as long as you're choosing the devil (ego), whether you are conscious of it or not, you are simultaneously rejecting God. Remember, in the Old Testament that Joshua challenged the tribe of Israel to wisely exercise the power of choice when he said, "Choose this day whom you will serve. As for me and my house, we shall serve the Lord."

Horse and carriage:

Imagine that your life is made up of you driving a horse and carriage. Now, imagine that one day, you are casually rolling along and a man with a gun pops out of the bushes. He points the gun at you, pulls out a whip, and demands that you get out of the carriage immediately. You get out of the carriage, and he proceeds to get in. Next, while still pointing the gun at you, he tells you to unhitch the horse and harness yourself in the horse's place. Scared for your life, you do as instructed.

Afterwards, he cracks the whip across your back and shoulders forcing you to do the work of the horse and pull him along the road. You quickly become exhausted, hurt, frustrated, and miserable, but continue to toil because you are very much afraid and don't want to lose your life (so you think). After a long while, you come across another man standing in the middle of the road blocking your way. He too has a gun and is pointing it directly at you. He commands you to stop. All the while, the other man that took you hostage is commanding you to go and is still cracking the whip. Completely depleted of everything (energy & strength – physically, mentally, emotionally drained) you decide to give up. You close your eyes and expect the worse. You are startled by a gunshot. A few seconds pass by, and you open your eyes to discover that you are ok. You look behind you and find that the man that was in the carriage has jumped out and run down the road in the direction (past) that you came from. You watch until he disappears over the horizon. What's more astonishing is that the man you just met in the middle of the road whistles. You hear the sound of galloping hooves and look again back to the direction from whence you came; lo and behold, it's your horse! The man then proceeds to re-hitch the horse to the carriage. Next, he jumps into the driver's seat. Your first inclination is that you are now going to be stranded on the side of the road, but wait; he motions for you to get up into the carriage and prepares a very comfortable place for you to sit. Finally, he proceeds to drive you from here on out, while you sit back, relax, and take in

178

the beautiful countryside without any cares or worries. Turns out that this man knows the territory like the back of his hand, and he knows where all the rough and dangerous spots are, so he avoids them. From here on out, your journey is smooth; you are safe, secure, and happy. During the course of your newly acquired lifestyle, your new driver explains to you that the man who made you his slave was pointing an unloaded gun at you. If you had called his bluff, you would've known. You made a choice to suffer, and it was all for nothing; however, because you decided to finally (out of desperation) surrender, that was the equivalent of giving him permission to banish your evil oppressor once and for all so that you can finally live the good life. He also explains to you that he appeared when he did because you were on the verge of collapsing, but you could've made up your mind even before you became exhausted and refused to do the evil one's bidding. He goes on to say that at whatever time the refusal came, it would have caused him to appear right then and there, even if you would've refused at the time you were first hijacked. This is the way life is for most. The evil oppressor wielding the unloaded gun is the devil (ego). The good man in middle of the road with the loaded weapon (real power) represents God (conscious awareness). Choose God once and for all.

The devil's spell:

Choosing God also means breaking the devil's spell. Break the devil's spell by paying attention to how you swing back and forth (mentally). Notice one day you are happy and excited. Notice that at other times, you are bitter, resentful, fearful, or melancholy. If you are really paying attention, you will notice that these emotions come and go based upon your perception of what is happening to you and around you in the outer world. If you notice this much without fretting about it, then you are beginning to shake things up a little in the kingdom of hell. Next, notice how, maybe even on a daily basis, your mind goes from thinking about the past (whether it's fretting or joyfully reminiscing or worrying about and anticipating the future). Then see the pain and anguish this causes. You are now tilting the devil's throne, and he will frantically cling so as not to be ejected, but you must keep looking in spite of the anxiety that arises. Also, notice how you zone out; perhaps you are sitting in a waiting room or in your car waiting for the traffic signal to change; you then proceed to go into the abyss: a mental zone where there is nothing in particular by way of thought sights or thought sounds, but you forget that you exist. You are literally in a trance. Snap yourself out of it. Bring your mind's awareness back to the present moment. Pay attention to whatever is happening in the present as it is happening. Don't allow yourself to be lured back into the devil's spell. Finally, notice how you easily get sucked back into hell even though you intended to keep yourself in the present moment. How long did it take for you to notice that you went back to hell (the abyss: mental imaginings: negative emotions: unawareness: fantasizing or worrying over the future: regretting or reminiscing the past) since the last time you brought yourself back to the present? Was it a few minutes, hours, days? Don't worry. You may even notice that as you snap yourself out of it, you immediately are drawn back while imagining that you are aware. This is the way it goes in the beginning. This is good and normal progress. Just keep snapping yourself out of it as often as you can remember, and sooner or later (depending on your personal effort and diligence) you will get out of hell.

How to choose God:

Begin to look at your thoughts. Don't try to change, control, suppress, or manipulate them. Simply look. Refuse to get caught up in the devil's spell by recognizing it when it is upon you. If you are self absorbed in negative thought, then you are being carried away to hell which is what the devil wants. Self absorption is not to be confused with conscious seeing. Look at your thoughts, imaginings, and mental processes on a daily basis. Have a song stuck in your head? That's ok; consciously listen to it. That is all there is to it: no intellectual thought, pondering, reflection, or examination required about what you see or hear. Just look, listen, and leave it at that. Make it a daily habit to consciously look at and listen to your mind's inner workings. After a period of time, something very profound will happen. It can even be termed as a "revelation." You will see, perhaps for the first time, that you are not the person that you thought you were. You will see that the person you thought you were is not you at all; you'll see that it was your imaginary self image (ego) of what you were hypnotized to believe in. You'll begin to see that there is a different you that truly has nothing to do with the devil (ego). It may be a small glimpse at first but as you continue to (consciously) watch and listen to your mind's activity, that small glimpse that may have occurred for 2 seconds will turn into 2 minutes, then an hour, next a day, and finally, you are forever with God everyday, month after month, year after year. Bringing your self awareness to the present moment is the same thing as choosing God.

Useful and useless thought:

Thought and imagination in and of itself is not bad. It is potentially very good and a gift from God. It is the way of usage that causes suffering or brings joy. There are two kinds of thinking: useful thinking and useless thinking. Useful thinking is a necessity. It is employed in everyday life; it is implemented in order to get dressed, brush your teeth, and prepare to start your day. A student uses it to get his homework done. A mother uses it to prepare a meal for her family. Useless thought is also a factor that most people follow up with useful thought. While preparing to start your day, you wonder if traffic will be stalled. While doing homework the student frets over an upcoming test. While preparing the family meal, a mother worries that her husband won't be home in time for dinner. Take a mental inventory and think about your thoughts. As you go through them say to yourself, hmmm... that was a useless thought or hey, that was useful thinking. Do this without emotional reaction, and at some point, all useless thinking will cease, leaving you at peace with God and useful thought only.

Salvation Rejected:

A word to Christians on salvation rejected: based on the author's personal experience:
I used to be one of those Christians that repetitively went the altar confessing my sins and rededicating my life to Christ. Every time, I did it, I walked away with a sense of relief, but that relief was always short lived. Something inside of me always and instinctively knew that something was wrong. I intuitively knew that claiming the salvation of Christ was only the beginning. I suspected that there was more to it than just voicing it. I just didn't know what the missing link was. This is why I would constantly backslide and go straight back to hell. Then through a series of circumstances (most of them painful), I was led to the answer.
"Acceptance of the salvation of Christ" is more than just lip service. It means to reject the devil (ego). Most people will say, "Well, duhhh: it doesn't take a genius to know this," but those very people who think that they know are truly unaware of the real nature of evil that is the devil. I was unknowingly rejecting the very salvation that I had asked for by clinging to my ego and its self centered egotistical (evil) ways. As I walk amongst Christians, I can easily see that this is very prevalent. In a nutshell, the ego is of the devil and we are asking for salvation (deliverance) and

wanting to bring the devil (ego) with us into the Kingdom of Heaven. Again, it doesn't work that way. This is why I believe that most Christians believe that they are saved but have made hell their dwelling place. They refuse to give up their egos (not knowing that it is the devil) therefore re-condemning themselves which translates to rejecting the salvation of Christ. This is a most sinister trick that the devil has devised. Under no circumstances can you get into Heaven if you refuse to leave the devil. The Bible says that it is through faith, not works that you are saved, but you have to start somewhere. Begin with action (works). Make it a daily spiritual duty to reject the devil's instruction at least once a day. If you can do it more than once, then well and good. Refuse that angry retort that is the urging of the devil and consciously watch how you feel about it. Don't follow through with any passive aggressive tendencies; just be still and alertly observe how your ego demands and scream that you seek retribution. Here is the ultimate: step outside of yourself and look at the uncertainty that runs rampant in your mind telling you that it's time to rededicate yourself because you have fallen back into your sinful ways. Then realize that you never fell back because you never gave up your sinful ways (ego). This is the way to real acceptance that will eventually advance you all the way to the Kingdom of God. Here is an interesting tidbit: The label of "Christian" often times serve to keep the ego in place.

I AM Speaks: Investigate the devil:

My child, until you are able to see through the devil, you will never be able to see God/I AM. Until you cease your acquaintance with evil, you can never truly know Me. Stop going along with the devil's lies that you know Me. How can you, being so timid and afraid, claim to know Me? Let go of your circus acts of nobility, faith, and humility. Drop your foolish desire to appear righteous and pious among men. Don't you know that any attempt to impress another human is idol worship? There is no difference to Me between this type of idol worship and the devil worshiping of a satanic cult. It is all the same and will lead you straight to hell. You must be bold enough to call the devil's bluff. You must look at the devil head on with out flinching. I assure you that the devil has no power, but you must discover this for yourself. When will you start trusting Me and stop believing the devil? You must be like the child who finally decided to look into the closet and discovered that there was no monster after all. Yes, he was certainly afraid, but he made up his mind to investigate in spite of his fear. He decided to simply look and see for himself. He slowly and nervously approached the closet door. He gently clutched the door knob and all the while his hand was trembling. In a moment of intense anxiety, he flung open the door and what he saw was truly astonishing; he saw all his fears melt away in an instant. Stop attributing power and strength to the devil. You tell others that you don't, but I know that you do, and you know that you do. The fact that you have a fearful mind proves it. Your compulsive counterproductive behavior tells all. You tell others that you have defeated the devil and are strong in the Lord, but you continue to do his (the devil's) will. The way you treat yourself and your fellow man proves it, especially on a mental level. I see all, and your actions and fearful state of mind is evidence of your self lies. Yes, you are a frightened creature. Those that fear anything in life belong to the devil. You'd rather keep fostering the lies to protect your phony self image instead doing the right thing and turning to Me no matter what others think. Forget what other people think; ignore the lies and foolish thoughts that the devil whispers into your mind. The Bible says, "Resist the devil and he will flee from you." The way to resist is to dare to look at him. Exposure is the only way to extract him from your life once and for all. Dare to stand face to face with the devil and you will see that everything you accepted as truth was a lie. You will discover that what you assumed to be lies was in fact truth. Investigate evil and you will finally see what's real. Look at the devil and not only will he disappear, but you will finally behold and truly know Me (The Lord your God).

No one has all the answers:

No one (human being) has all the answers. Of course you know that, but you still continue to search for that special someone who will rescue you and solve all of your problems. Maybe it's your pastor, maybe its that special man or woman that you believe is your soul mate and will complete you, maybe its the president of the country, or maybe even the Messiah, but wait, hasn't the Messiah already rescued you? If He has, then why are you still desperately searching? Why are you still nervous and apprehensive? If you are truly saved (having received salvation) then why is your mind such a haunted house of horrors? Drop the notion that you are saved. If you want real salvation, I, the Lord your God, will give it to you, but you must let go of your theatrical performances and dismiss the devil once and for all. All the answers you desire exist, but you must cease your search for them and allow them to simply come to you. They can and they will. All you have to do is consistently listen to and abide in Me (God) for a change. All the answers (My Supreme Wisdom) are already within you. I repeat, no one on earth has all the answers (for your life's purpose), no one but you.

Out of options:

You must run out of options, and I will intervene. You must realize that all your mentally induced answers solve nothing. See that your intellect keeps you running in circles. Your solutions are based upon memorized past experiences that have not aided you thus far. Your ego can do nothing for you besides keep you in (spiritual) bondage. See the futility in seeking identity in worldly pursuits. Do this, and I will rescue you. See that it is the devil inspiring you to be driven on behalf of the world. Even when you do the right thing, see that it is your own self righteous attitude that is the source of motivation. Put a stop to the mental scrambling and neurotic chasing. Break the hypnotic spell of your repetitious mechanical thought and behavior. You must truly run out of options. I know that you can sense that you have run out of options which is why you've become desperate and repeat the same useless solutions over and over and over (compulsive behavior and destructive habits that are attempts to keep yourself busy and distracted). Let go of it all. Give it all up this instant, and I will help you because you've finally run out of options.

Where is God?

No doubt that you've heard, God is Omnipresence. God in within me; God is outside me; God is all around me: everywhere present. If this is the case then why do I miss the mark? Why am I not experiencing God and His goodness? Why is my mind so plagued with doubt and fear? If God is all over, then why does it seem as if He's so far away and not where I need Him to be: in the midst of my mind? Nature constantly renews and heals itself because of the presence of God, but why doesn't my mind follow suit? Here is the paradox. God is everywhere; He even dwells within the mind; but He is behind the veil. To experience the renewing of the mind, to obtain mental healing and spiritual balance, the veil must be rent, removed, and cast away.

The Veil:

The ego, the false sense of self, the phony self image, the neurotic mind, fear, the devil, the noisy mindset, incessant negative thought, persistent worries and aggravation, mechanical thinking, compulsive imaginings, depression, contrived happiness, sense of futility and hopelessness, the list goes on and proves that man is so divided and confused that he cannot recognize that he himself (his faulty mind) is the veil. The veil is the negatively conditioned mind of man. This is what prevents contact with the Higher Power that is God. Remove the veil, and there is God.

True Mental Conditioning:

Removing the veil is not what you think it is. The veil, being the ego self/the negatively conditioned mind must be extirpated (cast out). A negatively conditioned mind cannot be cured with positive conditioning because with a positively conditioned mind, comes the belief in its opposite which is the negative. With this line of reasoning comes the notion that fighting and struggling is a necessary part of the process. You are thinking that the positive must do battle with or overcome the negative. The struggle never ends, and the need for positive conditioning will never cease. Negativity will always rear its ugly head and try to sneak in. As a result, positivity will always have to be summoned to do battle with negativity. Back and forth we go: remember that the battle is over and has been won by God via Christ. Nothing positive can result from having to battle. It is an exhausting process. It drains your mental energy and keeps you weak, weary, and worried. There is another type of mental conditioning that has nothing to do with positive or negative. As a matter of fact, it's not really conditioning. It can be considered as de-conditioning. Dropping both the positive and negative mindset and returning to the natural mindset. In this natural mindset, the devil has no influence because this mindset is the dwelling place of the Spirit that is God Himself. It is the secret place of the Most High where you too can dwell. In this secret place, there is only peace of mind, true security, contentment, and bliss. This is what God has to offer (for God has not given us a spirit of fear but of a sound mind): Holy Bible. Dissolution of the ego is the only true mental conditioning.

Insight:

When some people think of insight, the imagination tends to kick in and see it as something strange and mysterious. It is viewed as something obtained only by certain people known commonly as philosophers, oracles, prophets, psychics, and such. Since the average individual is not considered one of the elite few on the previous list, then insight is considered unobtainable by the average. The notion is that you have to be favored of God to receive this special gift. Nothing could be further from the truth.
All are favored of God. Insight is not mysterious or complicated and everyone has it. Insight means to

see from within; this is done with awareness: awareness is **the spiritual being** of the individual; it **is the entity that is perceived inside the head that is peering out at the world from behind the eyeballs**. It is the self of the individual that is not the body or the mind. It is the One that sees from within. The only issue with insight that most people have is that it has been inverted. Seeing from without instead of seeing from within is the only problem. Viewing people and circumstances from the viewpoint of imagination or a conditioned mind instead of simply being aware of conditions and circumstances is the reason for all of the turmoil in any individual's life. Simply put, to be aware is the same as having insight.

Understanding:

There is a common misconception about understanding that most people have with regard to spirituality. It largely has to do with the intellect or intellectual understanding. Intellectual understanding and spiritual understanding are not the same. The average Joe can quote the golden rule. He has it memorized and has an intellectual feel for what it means: treat others like you want to be treated. This isn't real understanding from a spiritual standpoint. He may also have this intellectual understanding and even practices the golden rule, but in his mind he is being prodded with all sorts of resentful thoughts like, "this person doesn't deserve it or why should I have to yield." He practices the rule but internally he feels burdened by it. This is because the concept is just swimming around in his head but hasn't penetrated through to his emotional body. Spiritual understanding is more than just head knowledge. A person understands a truth when it not only is received fully by the mind but by the emotions (the heart) as well. Once the perceived truth is accepted by the emotions, it becomes second nature to the person. He doesn't have to think about or remind himself to practice the rule. He doesn't do it from a troublesome sense of Christian duty. He does it because it is now truly a part of him. Most importantly, he feels good about it because now he can truly see why and how the rule benefits him. He doesn't get upset over other people who may try and take advantage or not do their part. If he has to say "no" to someone, he doesn't feel any guilt whatsoever because it was the right thing to do. At times he is stern with others and yet maintains compassion. Its called being "Christlike." Others will sense something different about him and gravitate toward his (internal) strength. He happily lives his life according to his spiritual nature; he realizes that he is truly secure in the salvation of Christ and knows that God will handle all (worldly details).

Unfortunately the difference between spiritual and intellectual understanding is not explained in most churches; this is one of many reasons why its members continue to suffer hardships and conflict. Can't blame the church leaders for the dilemma because they also lack true understanding. The leaders themselves are suffering. Even more tragic is that man continues to substitute the false understanding for the real. Even in the wake of disastrous consequences, he stubbornly clings to his false understanding. What can be done is to see the suffering and investigate it. If properly investigated, then the golden rule or any other truth can become a part of any human being thereby uplifting him spiritually, mentally, and physically.

I AM is not a name but a state of Being:

The Bible says that when Moses asked, "What shall I tell them when they ask Who You Are." The answer was, "I AM." Tell them that "I AM" sent you." This is the only possible answer that could've been given. The Almighty Infinite One cannot be named, labeled, or categorized. God couldn't have given Moses a name such as "Charlie" because to have given a name would mean to establish an ego. God is pure Being or Spirit. God is without ego. To place an ego on God would mean to place limits on God (His knowledge, His power, His presence). This would mean that God would cease to be Holy (Whole and Complete within Himself). God would become divided and truly separated from man (in reality as opposed to imaginary separation) and the rest of the physical and mental universe. There would truly be chaos; the universe would be without law and order; nothing would make sense; it would disintegrate. God would cease to be Eternal and would not exist; creation couldn't have occurred; you, everything, and everyone you know couldn't exist.

"I AM" is the name that God told Moses, but in truth, it isn't really a name. It is an eternal state of being, existence, or awareness which is the same thing as self sustaining and eternal life (the eternal now). "I AM" is your spirit or point of awareness that is meshed with God's Awareness and is the eternal you. This (your awareness that is meshed with God's) is what makes you eternal. Jesus was trying to make it more understandable for human level wisdom by calling God, His Father. By doing this He was able to establish (to mankind) a better sense of Who and What God is without placing limits on God. Biologically speaking, you come from your father, and your dna plus other attributes are the same as your biological father's. Jesus was cluing us in (by calling God the Father) that we have inherited the same attributes (from God) just like we inherit from our fathers on a biological level. The most significant trait being eternal life. Unfortunately, man has an ego and took Christ's teachings out of context; arrogant and devil minded church leaders began to require their congregations to call them "father" as well, thereby instilling fear and mass confusion into their congregations. Now they believe in their mortality as opposed to their eternal natures because they see these earthly priests called "fathers" catching diseases, sinning, and dying just like everyone else. This equates to blasphemy and is a betrayal of the Universal One. These power hungry hypocrites are part of the reason why most Christians have little or no faith and are minions of the devil. Even though the scriptures clearly state that Christ warned, "call no man father," It is blatantly ignored by these church officials and their congregations, all for the purpose of making themselves gods and being worshipped by the masses. Jesus referred to God alone as Father. Congregations know this, but through the power of suggestion and mental association, (brainwashing) they equate these weak human figures and clergymen to gods and are not even aware of what they are doing. The masses go along with it because of their need to have something tangible (physical) to place their trust in. Trusting in that which is intangible is utterly confusing to mass Christianity although few will admit it. The irony of it all is that if the ego is dropped, then the real God becomes tangible. What's even more amazing is that the masses don't wake up and see that these are egotistical ordinary men that possess hardly any faith and no power in and of themselves. Even Jesus Christ said, "I myself can do nothing; it is the Father within that doeth the works." These so called men of God come into the world, age, get sick, and die just like everyone else. Apparently, Christ knew what would happen if labels of the sort where given to men. "I AM" is all that is seen and unseen and there can be no limits (labels) placed on Spirit.

Book VIII Reflections:

1. Investigate the devil, and you will find that he is not real.
2. No one has all the answers, but you can receive all the answers you need.
3. You must run out of options to receive help from God.
4. God is waiting for you behind the veil.
5. The spiritual veil is the ego.
6. Real mental conditioning is removing the veil that is the ego.
7. True insight is seeing from within or awareness; there is nothing complicated or mysterious about it.
8. Intellectual understanding and spiritual understanding are not the same.
9. I AM is not a label but a state of being.

The ego, fear, and, negativity: the unholy trinity:

They all go hand in hand. They are all the same. Fear is negativity. The ego is negativity. The ego is fear. It is the true antichrist or unholy trinity. They are the unholy father (ego), the unholy son (negativity), and the unholyghost (fear). One cannot exist without the other. Without fear, there would be no ego or negativity. Without the ego there would be no fear or negativity. Without negativity, there would be no fear or ego. Conquer one and the others collapse and disappear. This unholy trinity is the cause of all human error and suffering. It is the reason that the average Christian still insists on calling himself an unworthy sinner all the while praying to God. God does not deal with the unworthy, (John: 9:31) just ask the devil. Remember? Christ rebuked the devil. God only focuses on what is worthy. It is because of this evil trio that worldly events and circumstances continue to get worse. This is why the average individual has self-esteem issues and identity crises. Men think that they are women and vice versa. It is why one man considers himself superior to others and the other man considers himself inferior. It causes men to feel that they must conquer other men through various contests including war. Because of this awful and fake entity, people continue to ask, "Where is God? Why doesn't God intervene?" God has not turned His back on humanity. Humanity has turned on God. Humanity has shunned the Real God and enthroned a fake god (the ego) in His place. The world has no choice but to continue to get worse as long as the ego continues to be the god of mankind. Awareness is the only solution. Awareness is true seeing. Seeing that the ego is mechanical imagination will dissolve it and eventually put you back in right standing with God Himself. Seeing that fear is a false solution is another way. See that fear is a reaction that the ego tells you to perpetrate as a solution to deal with your present circumstances, but you must see it as totally bogus and ineffective. No matter what label you put on the negative emotion, see it as being fear and a wrong solution. Keep telling yourself this whether you think you believe it or not. Deep down you really do. It is truth and the ego/devil cannot stand against truth. This will cause the ego to loose its psychological hold on you so that God can give you real solutions. A third way is to see that negativity is also not the answer. It is the ego's method of staying alive. See it and then refuse to give in to it. Don't obey the ego's negative suggestions. This may cause anxiety at first but continue to disobey. Make it a habit of being disobedient to the negative ego and it will begin to starve to death and eventually die. This is exactly how Christ defeated satan in the wilderness. You really don't have the ability to be truly obedient to the Real God because you don't know how. For as it says in the scriptures, (paraphrase) "First the comforter must come and will teach you all spiritual things and truth." It is the ego that prevents the coming of the "comforter," and this is why you do not know how to consistently obey God. Even though you think that you do on an intellectual level. The ego has been in control for so long and has become so powerful that it causes you to get frustrated, bitter, and resentful when trying to thwart it. So called righteous behaviors and actions that accompany a negative mindset is not Real Obedience. It is ego obedience and does you no good. Real Obedience is putting forth a conscious effort in disobeying the ego which translates to obeying God. Habitual disobeying the ego will eventually kill it. Once the ego dies, there is God in all of His Glorious Splendor.

Daily prayer:

Say this prayer everyday if possible; commit it to memory; recite it before going to bed at night and upon awakening in the morning. It is the True Will of God. It is the prayer of Truth, and since it is Truth, there can be no vain repetition. (This can be accepted because it is referring to the Real You: not the ego self.)

God's will for me is that I may have Life and have it more abundantly. This is according to Christ. This means that God's will for me is Perfect Love, radiant health, wealth, happiness, and a sound, peaceful, fearless mind. God's Will is done in my mind, body, and circumstances. Life is good to me and good for me. I love all of Life and Life loves me. Life supports me generously. Life provides me with everything that I need in excess and overflowing. I am completely unified with myself, God, and the entire Universe because in reality, We are One. This was the declaration of Christ. There is absolutely nothing to fear in the entire Universe because We are One. How can I fear what I am unified with? I am absolutely confident at every level of my being (mind, body, and spirit). Most of all, God's will is that I dwell with Him in His Kingdom even on the earthly plane. I do not have to experience physical death of the body to enter the Kingdom for Christ said, "the Kingdom is right here, right now, within me (in my heart) and among us all (surrounding us)." I am totally fearless under all circumstances and possess absolute faith in my God, in the name of Christ. Amen.

Conclusion:

There is only One: One Spirit, One Life, One God. This Life is the life of everything that lives and breathes. It is the Life of all that can be seen, heard, and felt. This One Spirit is the Power that animates all fleshly bodies, causes all the planets and stars to orbit on a grand scale, and causes all subatomic particles to rotate on a microscopic scale. This is the One God, I AM, Who revealed Himself to Moses, and is the Father of Christ Jesus and all others. This One God is the unseen One Who created everything that is seen from His very Being. He dwells within and around everything that exists. He is everything that exists. Mankind may have individualized fleshly bodies and minds, but the Spirit upon which these minds and bodies operate is the One Spirit. This is why Christ said, "I and the Father are One." You too must come to this realization. Realization of your Oneness with God equates to being fearless.

GOD BLESS

25165652R00115

Made in the USA
San Bernardino, CA
20 October 2015